Wellne**S**s

Positive **M**otivational quotes

H**A**bit Tracking

Plan

High Pe**R**formance

Produc**T**ivity

Lif**E** gratitude

Proc**R**astination

"Mindfulness is deliberately paying full attention to what is happening around you- in your body, heart, and mind. Mindfulness is awareness without criticism or judgement

-- Jan Chozen Bays --

This Planner belongs to:

Introduction

Welcome to the Positive Productivity, Mindfulness, Self-Care, and Wellness Planner! The book that's going to make you more productive than a caffeinated squirrel on a mission.

Inside, you'll find all sorts of nifty tools to help you slay your to-do list, stay mindful, and practice self-care like a boss. From life goal-setting to daily planning, this planner has got you covered - and let's be real, it's way cuter than those boring, plain notebooks. Plus, this planner isn't just about getting things done — it's about taking care of yourself too.

Just remember to take it one step at a time and be kind to yourself.

Plenty of pages in case you change your mind and you like to add something different. All organised to be easy for you to find and to see your journey.

Use the prompts to help you with ideas for the last pages that you can use as a diary or more planning if it was not enough in the Time Planning Madness.

So, what are you waiting for? Grab your favorite pen (or pencil, or crayon, we don't judge), and let's start making magic happen. Because you, my friend, are destined for greatness.

Thanks a million for being part of our journey and for letting us be a part of your journey!

We hope you're absolutely loving this Planner and that it's making your life a bit easier and a hole lot happier!

If you've been enjoying your experience, we'd be absolutely thrilled if you could leave us a lovely review. It's like a little virtual hug that makes us feel warm and fuzzy inside! Plus, your feedback helps us improve, serve you better and let us and other know that we're doing something right!

But wait, there's more! We're always looking for ways to make our products and services even more amazing. So if you have any mind-blowing ideas or suggestions, please let us know. Our team of mad scientists will analyse every idea under a microscope, and who knows, maybe we'll come up with something truly revolutionary!

*Contact us directly to get some cute **free stickers** for your new planner!*
(UK only - check the last page for details)

Thanks for being an awesome customer!
May your day be filled with sunshine, rainbows and unicorns!

Mirela A S Tipping

Contents:

Serious Stuff:

Introduction 4
Thank you 5
Growth vs fixed mindset 9
Self-Assessment 10
Self-score Inventory 12
4 -7 - 8 Breathing Technique 14
5 4 3 2 1 Coping Technique 15
Vision Board 16
My intentions 22
Better Living 23
Self-Care Ideas 24
Me, Myself & I 30
My Why - Goals 32
Healthy Meals Ideas 38
Reward sheets 40
Procrastination tips 44

Time Planning Madness

To Do Lists 46
Daily Routine 54
Project Planner 56
Day on 1 page 64
Week on 2 pages 186
Month on 2 pages 238
Year on 1 page 262

Gratitude & Journal Prompts 264
Lined pages for Extra-Serious stuff 266
Calendar 2023 326
         2024
         2025
         2026

My Contents:

Add your own from the extra lined pages at the end.

8

STAY STRONG & POWER ON

Growth mindset and fixed mindset are like two little birds sitting on your shoulders, whispering in your ear. The growth bird chirps away, reminding you that with effort and hard work, you can improve and achieve anything you set your mind to.

The fixed bird, on the other hand, sits quietly and grumpily, telling you that your abilities are set in stone and you shouldn't bother trying too hard.

But here's the thing: the growth bird is way more fun to listen to! Embracing challenges, learning from mistakes, and pushing yourself to be better is way more exciting than giving up before you've even tried. So next time you hear those little birds chirping away, give the growth bird a big hug and tell them you're ready to soar to new heights!

GROWTH MINDSET	FIXED MINDSET
CHALLENGES Challenges are a way for me to get better	**CHALLENGES** I try to avoid challenges so i don't look stupid
DESIRES I'll try new things	**DESIRES** I'll just stick to what I know
SKILLS I can always improve	**SKILLS** I'm either good at it or not. If I'm not, it's okay
OBSTACLES I'll change my approach until I succeed	**OBSTACLES** I'm just not good at it and that's the way it is
SUCCESS OF OTHERS I'm inspired by their success.	**SUCCESS OF OTHERS** It's unfair that they're succeeding and I am not
CRITICISM I can learn from the feedback I receive	**CRITICISM** I feel threatened by the criticism I get

Self-Assessment

It's decision time: Choose wisely, because there's no turning back once you've made your choice! X in your choice ...

I eat healthy foods regularly

Disagree   Neutral   Agree

I get an adequate amount of sleep

Disagree   Neutral   Agree

I exercise regularly

Disagree   Neutral   Agree

I rest when I'm sick

Disagree   Neutral   Agree

I take enough time off work

Disagree   Neutral   Agree

I have hobbies and passions that I enjoy

Disagree   Neutral   Agree

I speak openly about my problems

Disagree   Neutral   Agree

I spend time with friends and family

Disagree   Neutral   Agree

I work on my personal growth

Disagree   Neutral   Agree

I feel grateful about many aspects of my life

Disagree   Neutral   Agree

I'm happy with my work

Disagree   Neutral   Agree

I work on my professional skills

Disagree   Neutral   Agree

Self-Assessment

Just kidding ... Come back when you think something had changed. Color in your choice or just mark it with an X or Y or any letter that you like :-) ...

I eat healthy foods regularly

Disagree   Neutral   Agree

I get an adequate amount of sleep

Disagree   Neutral   Agree

I exercise regularly

Disagree   Neutral   Agree

I rest when I'm sick

Disagree   Neutral   Agree

I take enough time off work

Disagree   Neutral   Agree

I have hobbies and passions that I enjoy

Disagree   Neutral   Agree

I speak openly about my problems

Disagree   Neutral   Agree

I spend time with friends and family

Disagree   Neutral   Agree

I work on my personal growth

Disagree   Neutral   Agree

I feel grateful about many aspects of my life

Disagree   Neutral   Agree

I'm happy with my work

Disagree   Neutral   Agree

I work on my professional skills

Disagree   Neutral   Agree

Level 10 Self-score Inventory

Taking the Level 10 Self-score Inventory is like giving yourself a little report card on how awesome you are! It's like a fun and friendly game of "Let's see how much of a rock-star I am at life!" It helps you take a step back and assess all the different areas of your life, from your relationships to your personal growth, and figure out where you're crushing it and where you could use a little boost. So, why not give it a try?

You might just find out you're a Level 10 superstar in disguise!

FAMILY/ FRIENDS	1	2	3	4	5	6	7	8	9	10
SELF DEVELOPMENT	1	2	3	4	5	6	7	8	9	10
SPIRITUALITY	1	2	3	4	5	6	7	8	9	10
FINANCES	1	2	3	4	5	6	7	8	9	10
CAREER	1	2	3	4	5	6	7	8	9	10
RELATIONSHIPS	1	2	3	4	5	6	7	8	9	10
RECREATION	1	2	3	4	5	6	7	8	9	10
GIVING	1	2	3	4	5	6	7	8	9	10
ENVIRONMENT	1	2	3	4	5	6	7	8	9	10
HEALTH	1	2	3	4	5	6	7	8	9	10

Come back with an update

FAMILY/ FRIENDS	1	2	3	4	5	6	7	8	9	10
SELF DEVELOPMENT	1	2	3	4	5	6	7	8	9	10
SPIRITUALITY	1	2	3	4	5	6	7	8	9	10
FINANCES	1	2	3	4	5	6	7	8	9	10
CAREER	1	2	3	4	5	6	7	8	9	10
RELATIONSHIPS	1	2	3	4	5	6	7	8	9	10
RECREATION	1	2	3	4	5	6	7	8	9	10
GIVING	1	2	3	4	5	6	7	8	9	10
ENVIRONMENT	1	2	3	4	5	6	7	8	9	10
HEALTH	1	2	3	4	5	6	7	8	9	10

4-7-8
Breathing technique

This breathing technique can aid relaxation and sleep. Start by sitting or lying in a comfortable position

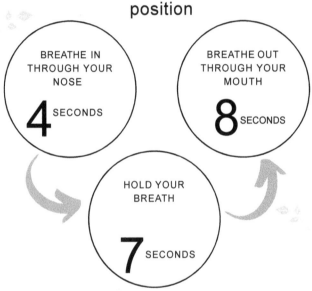

BREATHE IN
THROUGH YOUR
NOSE

4 SECONDS

BREATHE OUT
THROUGH YOUR
MOUTH

8 SECONDS

HOLD YOUR
BREATH

7 SECONDS

Repeat technique 4 times

PLEASE NOTE : IF YOU'RE NOT USED TO THIS BREATHING TECHNIQUE, IT CAN MAKE YOU FEEL LIGHT- HEADED, SO DON'T PRACTICE THIS WHILST DRIVING. IF YOU FEEL LIGHT - HEADED, TRY HALVING THE TIME AND BUILD UP TO 4 - 7- 8

5-4-3-2-1
Coping technique
For Anxiety

5 Acknowledge 5 things you see around you. It could be a pen, a spot on the ceiling, anything in your Soundings.

4 Acknowledge 4 things you can touch around you. It could be your hair, a pillow, or the ground under your feet.

3 Acknowledge 3 things you hear. This could be any external sound. If you can hear your belly rumbling that counts! Focus on things you can hear outside of your body.

2 Acknowledge 2 things you can smell. Maybe you are in your office and smell pencil, or maybe you are in your bedroom and smell a pillow. If you need to take a brief walk to find a scent you could smell soap in your bathroom, or nature outside.

1 Acknowledge 1 thing you can taste. What does the inside of your mouth taste like- gum, coffee, or the sandwich from lunch?

Are you feeling like you need a little direction in life? Well, don't worry, my friend. Writing a vision board can help you get your ducks in a row and achieve your goals. Here's how it can help in different areas:

Career: Write down your career aspirations, and let your imagination run wild! Maybe you'll discover that your true calling is to become a professional unicorn trainer, or a world - famous pizza critic.

Finance: Write down your financial goals, like saving up for that dream vacation or buying a fancy new car. Then take a look at your bank account and laugh at the absurdity of it all. Hey, at least you're trying!

Relationships/Love: Write down the qualities you're looking for in a partner, but don't be too picky. You might just discover that your soulmate is someone who likes to eat pizza in bed and watch Netflix all day.

Personal growth: Write down your personal growth goals, and give yourself a pat on the back for being such an ambitious and motivated person. Then take a nap, because all that self-reflection can be exhausting.

Health: Write down your health goals, like running a marathon or climbing a mountain. Then realise that you hate running and are scared of heights, and decide to take a nice long bubble bath instead.

Leisure: Write down the things you enjoy doing in your free time, whether it's painting, hiking, or binge-watching your favourite TV shows. Then go ahead and indulge in those activities guilt-free, because you deserve it!

Mindset: Write down positive affirmations and quotes that inspire you, and read them every morning to start your day off on the right foot. Then forget them all and eat some pizza, because let's be honest, that's always a good idea.

But in all seriousness, writing a vision board can help you visualise your goals and create a plan to achieve them. It can also help you stay motivated, focused, and accountable. So grab a pen and paper, and start writing your own vision board to help you achieve your dreams.

If you don't
TRY
You will never
KNOW!

PERSONAL GROWTH

HEALTH

LEISURE

MINDSET

PERSONAL GROWTH

BELIEVE IN YOURSELF

HEALTH

LEISURE

MINDSET

My intentions

Check in with yourself with clear intentions, built on a strong WHY. Sometime, we need to spend the time to really decide what this looks like for us. You can do that here. Don't be afraid to dream big!

WHERE AM I NOW?

WHERE DO I WANT TO BE?

WHY?

HOW CAN I BE BETTER?

WHAT STOPS ME FROM GETTING WHAT I WANT?

WHAT CAN HELP ME STAY MORE FOCUSED

Self-care ideas

*Self-care is like a secret love affair you have with yourself.
So go ahead and treat yourself. You'll feel ready to
conquer the world (or at least your laundry pile).
And don't worry, your secret is safe with me!*

TALK TO A FRIEND															
TELL SOMEONE YOU LOVE THEM															
WRITE YOUR JOURNAL															
REMEMBER YOU ARE AMAZING															
PLAY WITH YOUR PET															
DRINK MORE WATER															
WASH FACE & PUT ON A MASK															
EAT A HEALTHY MEAL															
LISTEN TO MUSIC															
DANCE LIKE NOBODY IS WATCHING															
DECLUTTER															
VISIT A FAVOURITE SPOT IN TOWN															
SELF FOOT RUB															
MOVE YOUR BODY AND EXERCISE															
PRACTICE DEEP BREATHING															
PRACTICE GRATITUDE															
PAINT / CLEAN YOUR NAILS															
REST - TAKE A NAP															
MEET WITH A FRIEND															
TAKE A NICE BUBBLE BATH															
LEARN SOMETHING NEW															
WATCH THE SUNRISE / SUNSET															
SMILE MORE (It's free)															
BUY YOURSELF SOME FLOWERS															

Self-care ideas

Why not add more? It is no such thing as too much Self-care! Mark each time you practice it and don't forget to reward yourself.

Self-care ideas

Go ahead and pamper yourself, whether it's taking a bubble bath or snuggling up with your pet.
You'll feel like a cozy burrito, wrapped up in a blanket of Self-love

TALK TO A FRIEND														
TELL SOMEONE YOU LOVE THEM														
WRITE YOUR JOURNAL														
REMEMBER YOU ARE AMAZING														
PLAY WITH YOUR PET														
DRINK MORE WATER														
WASH FACE & PUT ON A MASK														
EAT A HEALTHY MEAL														
LISTEN TO MUSIC														
DANCE LIKE NOBODY IS WATCHING														
DECLUTTER														
VISIT A FAVOURITE SPOT IN TOWN														
SELF FOOT RUB														
MOVE YOUR BODY AND EXERCISE														
PRACTICE DEEP BREATHING														
PRACTICE GRATITUDE														
PAINT / CLEAN YOUR NAILS														
REST - TAKE A NAP														
MEET WITH A FRIEND														
TAKE A NICE BUBBLE BATH														
LEARN SOMETHING NEW														
WATCH THE SUNRISE / SUNSET														
SMILE MORE (It's free)														
BUY YOURSELF SOME FLOWERS														

Self-care ideas

Self-care is like a magic potion that recharges your batteries. And we all know that ...
Nothing works with empty batteries!
Remember, a little self-care goes a long way!

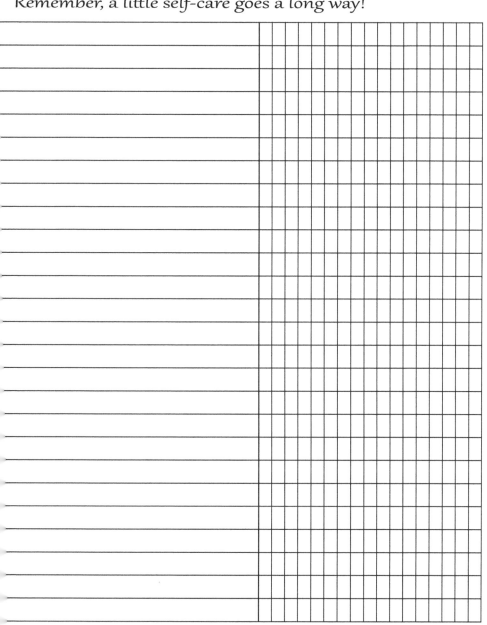

Self-care ideas

Taking care of yourself is not only necessary, but also a fun way to show yourself some love.

	M	T	W	T	F	S	S
TALK TO A FRIEND							
TELL SOMEONE YOU LOVE THEM							
WRITE YOUR JOURNAL							
REMEMBER YOU ARE AMAZING							
PLAY WITH YOUR PET							
DRINK MORE WATER							
WASH FACE & PUT ON A MASK							
EAT A HEALTHY MEAL							
LISTEN TO MUSIC							
DANCE LIKE NOBODY IS WATCHING							
DECLUTTER							
VISIT A FAVOURITE SPOT IN TOWN							
SELF FOOT RUB							
MOVE YOUR BODY AND EXERCISE							
PRACTICE DEEP BREATHING							
PRACTICE GRATITUDE							
PAINT / CLEAN YOUR NAILS							
REST - TAKE A NAP							
MEET WITH A FRIEND							
TAKE A NICE BUBBLE BATH							
LEARN SOMETHING NEW							
WATCH THE SUNRISE / SUNSET							
SMILE MORE (It's free)							
BUY YOURSELF SOME FLOWERS							

Self-care ideas

Make your own menu of treats for your well-being. It's like having your own self-care chef who knows exactly what you need to feel at your best

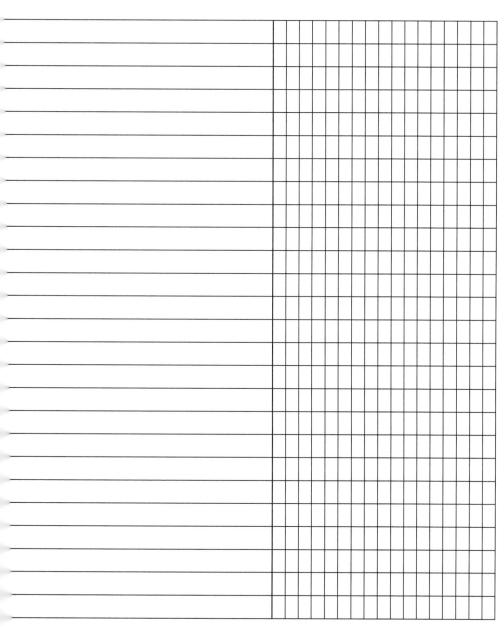

Daily affirmations

I am Loved!
I am amazing!
I can do anything!

Me, Myself & I

Daily affirmations

love

MY WHY

Write your reasons that will keep you motivated in the journey to your Goals or Habits here.

Workout

MY WHY

Write your reasons that will keep you motivated in the journey to your Goals or Habits here.

MY WHY

Write your reasons that will keep you motivated in the journey to your Goals or Habits here.

Write your reasons that will keep you motivated in the journey to your Goals or Habits here.

MY WHY

Write your reasons that will keep you motivated in the journey to your Goals or Habits here.

MY WHY

Write your reasons that will keep you motivated in the journey to your Goals or Habits here.

Healthy Meal Ideas

BREAKFAST	LUNCH	DINNER	SNACKS

BREAKFAST	LUNCH	DINNER	SNACKS

Reward Sheet

Reward yourself from time to time, for example every weekend/Month after you marked all the habits (in the weekly planner) you wanted to do.

Habit	Reward	When	
Running	Ice cream	Weekend	

Reward Sheet

Rewarding yourself is a great way to keep you motivated. Mark in the small boxes for each time you rewarded yourself too.

Habit	Reward	When							

Reward Sheet

Reward yourself from time to time, for example every weekend/Month after you marked all the habits (in the weekly planner) you wanted to do.

Habit	Reward	When								
Running	Ice cream	Weekend								

Reward Sheet

Rewarding yourself is a great way to keep you motivated.

Habit	Reward	When	

Break up your tasks into smaller, more manageable chunks. It will make it less overwhelming and easier to get started.

Create a to-do list and put a smiley face next to each task. It will make you feel happy and motivated to complete them.

Pretend that you're in a race against a cartoon character to finish your work. Make sure you win, or else you'll be beaten by a fictional character!

Tell yourself that you can have a treat after you finish each task. It will give you a sweet reward for your hard work.

Imagine that you're a superhero and your job is to save the day by completing your tasks. The fate of the world depends on you!

Turn on your favorite upbeat music and dance your way through your to-do list. You'll have fun while being productive.

Make a bet with a friend that you'll finish your work by a certain time. If you win, they owe you a treat. If you lose, you owe them one.

Set a timer for 10 minutes and challenge yourself to work on your task for that amount of time. You'll be surprised at how much you can get done in a short burst of focus.

Create a fun punishment for yourself if you don't complete your work on time. Maybe you have to wear a silly hat or do a funny dance in public.

Visualize how relieved you'll feel once your work is done. The feeling of accomplishment will be worth the effort.

Finally, remind yourself that procrastination only makes things worse in the long run. So, grab your work and get it done with a smile!

Time Planning Madness

TO DO LIST

TO DO LIST

TO DO LIST

- [ ]
- [ ]
- [ ]
- [ ]
- [ ]
- [ ]
- [ ]
- [ ]
- [ ]
- [ ]
- [ ]
- [ ]
- [ ]
- [ ]
- [ ]
- [ ]
- [ ]
- [ ]
- [ ]
- [ ]
- [ ]
- [ ]
- [ ]
- [ ]
- [ ]
- [ ]
- [ ]
- [ ]

TO DO LIST

TO DO LIST

- [ ]   [ ]
- [ ]   [ ]
- [ ]   [ ]
- [ ]   [ ]
- [ ]   [ ]
- [ ]   [ ]
- [ ]   [ ]
- [ ]   [ ]

- [ ]   [ ]
- [ ]   [ ]
- [ ]   [ ]
- [ ]   [ ]
- [ ]   [ ]
- [ ]   [ ]
- [ ]   [ ]
- [ ]   [ ]

- [ ]   [ ]
- [ ]   [ ]
- [ ]   [ ]
- [ ]   [ ]
- [ ]   [ ]
- [ ]   [ ]
- [ ]   [ ]
- [ ]   [ ]

TO DO LIST

- [ ]
- [ ]
- [ ]
- [ ]
- [ ]
- [ ]
- [ ]
- [ ]
- [ ]
- [ ]
- [ ]
- [ ]
- [ ]
- [ ]
- [ ]
- [ ]
- [ ]
- [ ]
- [ ]
- [ ]
- [ ]
- [ ]
- [ ]
- [ ]
- [ ]
- [ ]
- [ ]
- [ ]

TO DO LIST

- [ ]
- [ ]
- [ ]
- [ ]
- [ ]
- [ ]
- [ ]
- [ ]
- [ ]
- [ ]
- [ ]
- [ ]
- [ ]
- [ ]
- [ ]
- [ ]
- [ ]
- [ ]
- [ ]
- [ ]
- [ ]
- [ ]
- [ ]
- [ ]
- [ ]
- [ ]

Daily Routine

Mornings	Lunch

Evenings	Weekends

Project Planner

TITLE:

START DATE: | DUE DATE:

PROJECT GOALS & OBJECTIVES

BRAIN STORMING

ACTION STEPS

Notes:

Project Planner

TITLE:

START DATE: DUE DATE:

PROJECT GOALS & OBJECTIVES

BRAIN STORMING

ACTION STEPS

Notes:

Project Planner

TITLE:

START DATE:

DUE DATE:

PROJECT GOALS & OBJECTIVES

BRAIN STORMING

ACTION STEPS

Notes:

TITLE:

START DATE: | DUE DATE:

PROJECT GOALS & OBJECTIVES

BRAIN STORMING

ACTION STEPS

Notes:

Project Planner

TITLE:

START DATE: | DUE DATE:

PROJECT GOALS & OBJECTIVES

BRAIN STORMING

ACTION STEPS

Notes:

TITLE:

START DATE: | DUE DATE:

PROJECT GOALS & OBJECTIVES

BRAIN STORMING

ACTION STEPS

Notes:

Project Planner

TITLE:	
START DATE:	DUE DATE:

PROJECT GOALS & OBJECTIVES

BRAIN STORMING

ACTION STEPS

Notes:

Project Planner

TITLE:

START DATE: DUE DATE:

PROJECT GOALS & OBJECTIVES

BRAIN STORMING

ACTION STEPS

Notes:

Daily Planner

SCHEDULE

6:00

7:00

8:00

9:00

10:00

11:00

12:00

1:00

2:00

3:00

4:00

5:00

6:00

7:00

8:00

TO DO LIST

○
○
○
○
○
○
○
○

NOTES

DO IT YOUR SELF FOR

Daily Planner

SCHEDULE

6:00

7:00

8:00

9:00

10:00

11:00

12:00

1:00

2:00

3:00

4:00

5:00

6:00

7:00

8:00

TO DO LIST

○
○
○
○
○
○
○
○
○
○

The way to get started is to quit talking and begin doing.

-Walt Disney

NOTES

Daily Planner

SCHEDULE

6:00

7:00

8:00

9:00

10:00

11:00

12:00

1:00

2:00

3:00

4:00

5:00

6:00

7:00

8:00

TO DO LIST

○
○
○
○
○
○
○
○
○

Focus on the positive, let go of negativity.

NOTES

Daily Planner

SCHEDULE

6:00

7:00

8:00

9:00

10:00

11:00

12:00

1:00

2:00

3:00

4:00

5:00

6:00

7:00

8:00

TO DO LIST

○
○
○
○
○
○
○
○

> **"If your really want something, you'll find a way. If not, you find Excuses."**
> - Jim Rohn

NOTES

Daily Planner

SCHEDULE

6:00

7:00

8:00

9:00

10:00

11:00

12:00

1:00

2:00

3:00

4:00

5:00

6:00

7:00

8:00

TO DO LIST

○ _____
○ _____
○ _____
○ _____
○ _____
○ _____
○ _____
○ _____

LOVE YOURSELF

NOTES

Daily Planner

/ /

SCHEDULE

6:00

7:00

8:00

9:00

10:00

11:00

12:00

1:00

2:00

3:00

4:00

5:00

6:00

7:00

8:00

TO DO LIST

○
○
○
○
○
○
○
○

Say no to distractions, yes to productivity.

NOTES

Daily Planner

SCHEDULE

6:00

7:00

8:00

9:00

10:00

11:00

12:00

1:00

2:00

3:00

4:00

5:00

6:00

7:00

8:00

TO DO LIST

○
○
○
○
○
○
○
○

"If at first you don't succeed, redefine success."

- George Carlin

NOTES

Daily Planner

/ /

SCHEDULE

6:00

7:00

8:00

9:00

10:00

11:00

12:00

1:00

2:00

3:00

4:00

5:00

6:00

7:00

8:00

TO DO LIST

- ○
- ○
- ○
- ○
- ○
- ○
- ○
- ○
- ○

Life is too short
to take it
seriously.

NOTES

Daily Planner

SCHEDULE

6:00

7:00

8:00

9:00

10:00

11:00

12:00

1:00

2:00

3:00

4:00

5:00

6:00

7:00

8:00

TO DO LIST

○
○
○
○
○
○
○
○

Procaffeinating: the art of putting off until coffee.

NOTES

Daily Planner

SCHEDULE

6:00

7:00

8:00

9:00

10:00

11:00

12:00

1:00

2:00

3:00

4:00

5:00

6:00

7:00

8:00

TO DO LIST

○ _____
○ _____
○ _____
○ _____
○ _____
○ _____
○ _____
○ _____

Focus on progress, not perfection.

NOTES

Daily Planner

SCHEDULE

6:00

7:00

8:00

9:00

10:00

11:00

12:00

1:00

2:00

3:00

4:00

5:00

6:00

7:00

8:00

TO DO LIST

○
○
○
○
○
○
○
○

Believe in yourself, you've got this!

NOTES

Daily Planner

SCHEDULE

6:00

7:00

8:00

9:00

10:00

11:00

12:00

1:00

2:00

3:00

4:00

5:00

6:00

7:00

8:00

TO DO LIST

○

○

○

○

○

○

○

○

Your time is precious, waste it wisely!

NOTES

Daily Planner

SCHEDULE

6:00

7:00

8:00

9:00

10:00

11:00

12:00

1:00

2:00

3:00

4:00

5:00

6:00

7:00

8:00

TO DO LIST

○

○

○

○

○

○

○

○

○

DO YOUR THING

NOTES

Daily Planner

_/ _/

SCHEDULE

6:00

7:00

8:00

9:00

10:00

11:00

12:00

1:00

2:00

3:00

4:00

5:00

6:00

7:00

8:00

TO DO LIST

○
○
○
○
○
○
○
○

Why did the banana go to the doctor? It wasn't peeling well.

NOTES

Daily Planner

SCHEDULE

6:00

7:00

8:00

9:00

10:00

11:00

12:00

1:00

2:00

3:00

4:00

5:00

6:00

7:00

8:00

TO DO LIST

○ _____
○ _____
○ _____
○ _____
○ _____
○ _____
○ _____
○ _____
○ _____

When in doubt, add more coffee.

NOTES

Daily Planner

/ /

SCHEDULE

6:00

7:00

8:00

9:00

10:00

11:00

12:00

1:00

2:00

3:00

4:00

5:00

6:00

7:00

8:00

TO DO LIST

○
○
○
○
○
○
○
○

😊 😣 🙂 😠 😑 😞

My plan A didn't work, on to plan B: panic. :-)

NOTES

Daily Planner

SCHEDULE

6:00

7:00

8:00

9:00

10:00

11:00

12:00

1:00

2:00

3:00

4:00

5:00

6:00

7:00

8:00

TO DO LIST

○
○
○
○
○
○
○
○
○

Today's a new day, let's make it awesome.

NOTES

Daily Planner

/ /

SCHEDULE

6:00

7:00

8:00

9:00

10:00

11:00

12:00

1:00

2:00

3:00

4:00

5:00

6:00

7:00

8:00

TO DO LIST

- ◯
- ◯
- ◯
- ◯
- ◯
- ◯
- ◯
- ◯

BE
BRAVE

NOTES

Daily Planner

SCHEDULE

6:00

7:00

8:00

9:00

10:00

11:00

12:00

1:00

2:00

3:00

4:00

5:00

6:00

7:00

8:00

TO DO LIST

○

○

○

○

○

○

○

○

I woke up like this, ready to shine.

NOTES

Daily Planner

SCHEDULE

6:00

7:00

8:00

9:00

10:00

11:00

12:00

1:00

2:00

3:00

4:00

5:00

6:00

7:00

8:00

TO DO LIST

◯

◯

◯

◯

◯

◯

◯

◯

I plan to be more organised... tomorrow

NOTES

Daily Planner

SCHEDULE

6:00

7:00

8:00

9:00

10:00

11:00

12:00

1:00

2:00

3:00

4:00

5:00

6:00

7:00

8:00

TO DO LIST

○
○
○
○
○
○
○
○

NOTES

Daily Planner

SCHEDULE

6:00

7:00

8:00

9:00

10:00

11:00

12:00

1:00

2:00

3:00

4:00

5:00

6:00

7:00

8:00

TO DO LIST

○
○
○
○
○
○
○
○

Time to make things happen.

NOTES

Daily Planner

SCHEDULE

TO DO LIST

6:00

7:00

8:00

9:00

10:00

11:00

12:00

1:00

2:00

3:00

4:00

5:00

6:00

7:00

8:00

Wake up and chase your dreams.

NOTES

/__/

SCHEDULE

6:00

7:00

8:00

9:00

10:00

11:00

12:00

1:00

2:00

3:00

4:00

5:00

6:00

7:00

8:00

TO DO LIST

○
○
○
○
○
○
○
○

I'm not weird,
I'm just
Limited Edition.

NOTES

Daily Planner

SCHEDULE

6:00

7:00

8:00

9:00

10:00

11:00

12:00

1:00

2:00

3:00

4:00

5:00

6:00

7:00

8:00

TO DO LIST

- ◯
- ◯
- ◯
- ◯
- ◯
- ◯
- ◯
- ◯

Mornings are tough, but so are you!

NOTES

/ /

SCHEDULE

6:00

7:00

8:00

9:00

10:00

11:00

12:00

1:00

2:00

3:00

4:00

5:00

6:00

7:00

8:00

TO DO LIST

○
○
○
○
○
○
○
○

I plan therefore I nap. :-)

NOTES

Daily Planner

SCHEDULE

6:00

7:00

8:00

9:00

10:00

11:00

12:00

1:00

2:00

3:00

4:00

5:00

6:00

7:00

8:00

TO DO LIST

○
○
○
○
○
○
○
○
○

I'm not always right, but I'm never wrong. :-)

NOTES

Daily Planner

SCHEDULE

6:00

7:00

8:00

9:00

10:00

11:00

12:00

1:00

2:00

3:00

4:00

5:00

6:00

7:00

8:00

TO DO LIST

○

○

○

○

○

○

○

○

Visualize success. Imagine how good it will feel to finish.

NOTES

Daily Planner

SCHEDULE

6:00

7:00

8:00

9:00

10:00

11:00

12:00

1:00

2:00

3:00

4:00

5:00

6:00

7:00

8:00

TO DO LIST

○ ___
○ ___
○ ___
○ ___
○ ___
○ ___
○ ___
○ ___

Often & small breaks are the key to Big Success. ;-)

NOTES

Daily Planner

/__/

SCHEDULE

6:00

7:00

8:00

9:00

10:00

11:00

12:00

1:00

2:00

3:00

4:00

5:00

6:00

7:00

8:00

TO DO LIST

○
○
○
○
○
○
○
○

DO YOUR BEST

NOTES

Daily Planner

SCHEDULE

6:00

7:00

8:00

9:00

10:00

11:00

12:00

1:00

2:00

3:00

4:00

5:00

6:00

7:00

8:00

TO DO LIST

○
○
○
○
○
○
○
○

Eat.
Plan.
Sleep.
Repeat.

NOTES

Daily Planner

SCHEDULE

6:00

7:00

8:00

9:00

10:00

11:00

12:00

1:00

2:00

3:00

4:00

5:00

6:00

7:00

8:00

TO DO LIST

○
○
○
○
○
○
○
○

Make work a game to conquer.

NOTES

Daily Planner

SCHEDULE

6:00

7:00

8:00

9:00

10:00

11:00

12:00

1:00

2:00

3:00

4:00

5:00

6:00

7:00

8:00

TO DO LIST

○
○
○
○
○
○
○
○

Laugh often, it's the best medicine.

NOTES

Daily Planner

/ /

SCHEDULE

6:00

7:00

8:00

9:00

10:00

11:00

12:00

1:00

2:00

3:00

4:00

5:00

6:00

7:00

8:00

TO DO LIST

○
○
○
○
○
○
○
○

IF ALL ELSE
fails
TAKE A
nap

NOTES

Daily Planner

SCHEDULE

6:00

7:00

8:00

9:00

10:00

11:00

12:00

1:00

2:00

3:00

4:00

5:00

6:00

7:00

8:00

TO DO LIST

○
○
○
○
○
○
○
○

"Time may be a
great healer,
but it's a lousy
beautician."

- Dorothy Parker

NOTES

Daily Planner

/ /

SCHEDULE

6:00

7:00

8:00

9:00

10:00

11:00

12:00

1:00

2:00

3:00

4:00

5:00

6:00

7:00

8:00

TO DO LIST

○
○
○
○
○
○
○
○

Life is too short to wait for tomorrow.

NOTES

Daily Planner

SCHEDULE

6:00

7:00

8:00

9:00

10:00

11:00

12:00

1:00

2:00

3:00

4:00

5:00

6:00

7:00

8:00

TO DO LIST

◯
◯
◯
◯
◯
◯
◯
◯

What do you call an alligator wearing a vest? An investigator. :-)

NOTES

Daily Planner

SCHEDULE

6:00

7:00

8:00

9:00

10:00

11:00

12:00

1:00

2:00

3:00

4:00

5:00

6:00

7:00

8:00

TO DO LIST

○
○
○
○
○
○
○
○

**Success =
Luck +
Pretending to know.
:-)**

NOTES

Daily Planner

SCHEDULE

6:00

7:00

8:00

9:00

10:00

11:00

12:00

1:00

2:00

3:00

4:00

5:00

6:00

7:00

8:00

TO DO LIST

○
○
○
○
○
○
○
○
○

SMILE BREATHE AND GO slowly

NOTES

Daily Planner

/ /

SCHEDULE

6:00

7:00

8:00

9:00

10:00

11:00

12:00

1:00

2:00

3:00

4:00

5:00

6:00

7:00

8:00

TO DO LIST

○
○
○
○
○
○
○
○

You're doing better than you think!

NOTES

Daily Planner

/ /

SCHEDULE

6:00

7:00

8:00

9:00

10:00

11:00

12:00

1:00

2:00

3:00

4:00

5:00

6:00

7:00

8:00

TO DO LIST

○
○
○
○
○
○
○
○
○
○

I'm not perfect, but my pet thinks I am.

NOTES

Daily Planner

SCHEDULE

6:00

7:00

8:00

9:00

10:00

11:00

12:00

1:00

2:00

3:00

4:00

5:00

6:00

7:00

8:00

TO DO LIST

◯ _____

◯ _____

◯ _____

◯ _____

◯ _____

◯ _____

◯ _____

◯ _____

Be the reason someone smiles today... or drinks. :-)

NOTES

Daily Planner

SCHEDULE

6:00

7:00

8:00

9:00

10:00

11:00

12:00

1:00

2:00

3:00

4:00

5:00

6:00

7:00

8:00

TO DO LIST

○ _____
○ _____
○ _____
○ _____
○ _____
○ _____
○ _____
○ _____

LOVE your self FIRST

NOTES

Daily Planner

SCHEDULE

6:00

7:00

8:00

9:00

10:00

11:00

12:00

1:00

2:00

3:00

4:00

5:00

6:00

7:00

8:00

TO DO LIST

○
○
○
○
○
○
○
○

I'm just Fun-sized and Fabulous.

NOTES

Daily Planner

MTWTFSS
/ /

SCHEDULE

6:00

7:00

8:00

9:00

10:00

11:00

12:00

1:00

2:00

3:00

4:00

5:00

6:00

7:00

8:00

TO DO LIST

○
○
○
○
○
○
○
○

"Whoever is happy will make others happy too."

-Anne Frank

NOTES

Daily Planner

SCHEDULE

6:00

7:00

8:00

9:00

10:00

11:00

12:00

1:00

2:00

3:00

4:00

5:00

6:00

7:00

8:00

TO DO LIST

○
○
○
○
○
○
○
○

"Life itself is the most wonderful fairy tale."

-Hans Christian Andersen

NOTES

Daily Planner

SCHEDULE

6:00

7:00

8:00

9:00

10:00

11:00

12:00

1:00

2:00

3:00

4:00

5:00

6:00

7:00

8:00

TO DO LIST

○

○

○

○

○

○

○

○

DO IT YOUR SELF

NOTES

Daily Planner

/ /

SCHEDULE	TO DO LIST

SCHEDULE

6:00

7:00

8:00

9:00

10:00

11:00

12:00

1:00

2:00

3:00

4:00

5:00

6:00

7:00

8:00

TO DO LIST

○
○
○
○
○
○
○
○

"No pressure, No diamonds."

- Thomas Carlyle

NOTES

Daily Planner

SCHEDULE

6 : 0 0

7 : 0 0

8 : 0 0

9 : 0 0

10 : 0 0

11 : 0 0

12 : 0 0

1 : 0 0

2 : 0 0

3 : 0 0

4 : 0 0

5 : 0 0

6 : 0 0

7 : 0 0

8 : 0 0

TO DO LIST

○_____
○_____
○_____
○_____
○_____
○_____
○_____
○_____

"Life is ours to
be spent,
not to be saved."

-D. H. Lawrence

NOTES

Daily Planner

SCHEDULE

6:00

7:00

8:00

9:00

10:00

11:00

12:00

1:00

2:00

3:00

4:00

5:00

6:00

7:00

8:00

TO DO LIST

○
○
○
○
○
○
○
○

Start somewhere...

NOTES

Daily Planner

SCHEDULE

6:00

7:00

8:00

9:00

10:00

11:00

12:00

1:00

2:00

3:00

4:00

5:00

6:00

7:00

8:00

TO DO LIST

○ _____
○ _____
○ _____
○ _____
○ _____
○ _____
○ _____
○ _____
○ _____

LOVE YOURSELF

NOTES

Daily Planner

/ /

SCHEDULE

6:00

7:00

8:00

9:00

10:00

11:00

12:00

1:00

2:00

3:00

4:00

5:00

6:00

7:00

8:00

TO DO LIST

○
○
○
○
○
○
○
○

> ## "Don't let yesterday take too much of today."
> - Will Rogers

NOTES

Daily Planner

SCHEDULE

6:00

7:00

8:00

9:00

10:00

11:00

12:00

1:00

2:00

3:00

4:00

5:00

6:00

7:00

8:00

TO DO LIST

○
○
○
○
○
○
○
○

Today is the Beginning.

NOTES

Daily Planner

/ /

SCHEDULE

6:00

7:00

8:00

9:00

10:00

11:00

12:00

1:00

2:00

3:00

4:00

5:00

6:00

7:00

8:00

TO DO LIST

○
○
○
○
○
○
○
○

"When nothing goes Right, go Left."

- Martha Cecilia

NOTES

Daily Planner

SCHEDULE

6:00

7:00

8:00

9:00

10:00

11:00

12:00

1:00

2:00

3:00

4:00

5:00

6:00

7:00

8:00

TO DO LIST

Don't stop until you're proud!

NOTES

Daily Planner

SCHEDULE

6:00

7:00

8:00

9:00

10:00

11:00

12:00

1:00

2:00

3:00

4:00

5:00

6:00

7:00

8:00

TO DO LIST

○
○
○
○
○
○
○

"Failure is Success in progress."

- Albert Einstein

NOTES

Daily Planner

SCHEDULE

6:00

7:00

8:00

9:00

10:00

11:00

12:00

1:00

2:00

3:00

4:00

5:00

6:00

7:00

8:00

TO DO LIST

○
○
○
○
○
○
○
○
○

Positive mind. Positive vibes. Positive life.

NOTES

Daily Planner

/ /

SCHEDULE

6:00

7:00

8:00

9:00

10:00

11:00

12:00

1:00

2:00

3:00

4:00

5:00

6:00

7:00

8:00

TO DO LIST

○
○
○
○
○
○
○
○

Learn to rest Not to quit.

- Banksy

NOTES

Daily Planner

SCHEDULE

6:00

7:00

8:00

9:00

10:00

11:00

12:00

1:00

2:00

3:00

4:00

5:00

6:00

7:00

8:00

TO DO LIST

- ○
- ○
- ○
- ○
- ○
- ○
- ○
- ○

DO YOUR THING

NOTES

Daily Planner

SCHEDULE

6:00

7:00

8:00

9:00

10:00

11:00

12:00

1:00

2:00

3:00

4:00

5:00

6:00

7:00

8:00

TO DO LIST

○

○

○

○

○

○

○

○

"If you think you can
you can,
if you think you can't
you're right!"
— Abraham Lincoln

NOTES

Daily Planner

SCHEDULE

6:00

7:00

8:00

9:00

10:00

11:00

12:00

1:00

2:00

3:00

4:00

5:00

6:00

7:00

8:00

TO DO LIST

○

○

○

○

○

○

○

○

DO IT YOUR SELF

NOTES

Daily Planner

/ /

SCHEDULE

6:00

7:00

8:00

9:00

10:00

11:00

12:00

1:00

2:00

3:00

4:00

5:00

6:00

7:00

8:00

TO DO LIST

○
○
○
○
○
○
○
○

The way to get started is to quit talking and begin doing.
-Walt Disney

NOTES

Daily Planner

SCHEDULE

6:00

7:00

8:00

9:00

10:00

11:00

12:00

1:00

2:00

3:00

4:00

5:00

6:00

7:00

8:00

TO DO LIST

○ _____
○ _____
○ _____
○ _____
○ _____
○ _____
○ _____
○ _____
○ _____
○ _____

Focus on the positive, let go of negativity.

NOTES

Daily Planner

/ /

SCHEDULE

6:00

7:00

8:00

9:00

10:00

11:00

12:00

1:00

2:00

3:00

4:00

5:00

6:00

7:00

8:00

TO DO LIST

○ _____

○ _____

○ _____

○ _____

○ _____

○ _____

○ _____

○ _____

○ _____

"If your really want something, you'll find a way. If not, you find Excuses."

- Jim Rohn

NOTES

Daily Planner

SCHEDULE

6:00

7:00

8:00

9:00

10:00

11:00

12:00

1:00

2:00

3:00

4:00

5:00

6:00

7:00

8:00

TO DO LIST

○
○
○
○
○
○
○
○
○

LOVE YOURSELF

NOTES

Daily Planner

SCHEDULE

6:00

7:00

8:00

9:00

10:00

11:00

12:00

1:00

2:00

3:00

4:00

5:00

6:00

7:00

8:00

TO DO LIST

○

○

○

○

○

○

○

○

Say no to distractions, yes to productivity.

NOTES

Daily Planner

SCHEDULE

6:00

7:00

8:00

9:00

10:00

11:00

12:00

1:00

2:00

3:00

4:00

5:00

6:00

7:00

8:00

TO DO LIST

○
○
○
○
○
○
○
○

"If at first you don't succeed, redefine success."
- George Carlin

NOTES

Daily Planner

/ /

SCHEDULE

6:00

7:00

8:00

9:00

10:00

11:00

12:00

1:00

2:00

3:00

4:00

5:00

6:00

7:00

8:00

TO DO LIST

- ◯
- ◯
- ◯
- ◯
- ◯
- ◯
- ◯
- ◯

Life is too short to take it seriously.

NOTES

Daily Planner

SCHEDULE

6:00

7:00

8:00

9:00

10:00

11:00

12:00

1:00

2:00

3:00

4:00

5:00

6:00

7:00

8:00

TO DO LIST

○ _____
○ _____
○ _____
○ _____
○ _____
○ _____
○ _____
○ _____
○ _____

Procaffeinating: the art of putting off until coffee.

NOTES

Daily Planner

SCHEDULE

6:00

7:00

8:00

9:00

10:00

11:00

12:00

1:00

2:00

3:00

4:00

5:00

6:00

7:00

8:00

TO DO LIST

○
○
○
○
○
○
○
○

Focus on progress, not perfection.

NOTES

Daily Planner

SCHEDULE

6:00

7:00

8:00

9:00

10:00

11:00

12:00

1:00

2:00

3:00

4:00

5:00

6:00

7:00

8:00

TO DO LIST

○
○
○
○
○
○
○
○
○

Believe in yourself, you've got this!

NOTES

Daily Planner

SCHEDULE

6:00

7:00

8:00

9:00

10:00

11:00

12:00

1:00

2:00

3:00

4:00

5:00

6:00

7:00

8:00

TO DO LIST

- ◯
- ◯
- ◯
- ◯
- ◯
- ◯
- ◯
- ◯

Your time is precious, waste it wisely!

NOTES

Daily Planner

SCHEDULE

6:00

7:00

8:00

9:00

10:00

11:00

12:00

1:00

2:00

3:00

4:00

5:00

6:00

7:00

8:00

TO DO LIST

○ _____
○ _____
○ _____
○ _____
○ _____
○ _____
○ _____
○ _____
○ _____
○ _____

DO YOUR THING

NOTES

Daily Planner

/   /

SCHEDULE

6:00

7:00

8:00

9:00

10:00

11:00

12:00

1:00

2:00

3:00

4:00

5:00

6:00

7:00

8:00

TO DO LIST

○

○

○

○

○

○

○

○

Why did the banana go to the doctor? It wasn't peeling well.

NOTES

Daily Planner

SCHEDULE

6:00

7:00

8:00

9:00

10:00

11:00

12:00

1:00

2:00

3:00

4:00

5:00

6:00

7:00

8:00

TO DO LIST

○ _____
○ _____
○ _____
○ _____
○ _____
○ _____
○ _____
○ _____
○ _____

When in doubt, add more coffee.

NOTES

Daily Planner

SCHEDULE

6:00

7:00

8:00

9:00

10:00

11:00

12:00

1:00

2:00

3:00

4:00

5:00

6:00

7:00

8:00

TO DO LIST

○
○
○
○
○
○
○
○

My plan A didn't work, on to plan B: panic. :-)

NOTES

Daily Planner

SCHEDULE

TO DO LIST

6:00

○

○

7:00

○

○

8:00

○

○

9:00

○

○

10:00

○

11:00

12:00

**Today's a new day,
let's make it awesome.**

1:00

2:00

3:00

NOTES

4:00

5:00

6:00

7:00

8:00

Daily Planner

MTWTFSS

/ /

SCHEDULE

6:00

7:00

8:00

9:00

10:00

11:00

12:00

1:00

2:00

3:00

4:00

5:00

6:00

7:00

8:00

TO DO LIST

○

○

○

○

○

○

○

○

BE BRAVE

NOTES

Daily Planner

SCHEDULE

TO DO LIST

6:00

7:00

8:00

9:00

10:00

11:00

12:00

1:00

2:00

3:00

4:00

5:00

6:00

7:00

8:00

I woke up like this, ready to shine.

NOTES

Daily Planner

SCHEDULE

6:00

7:00

8:00

9:00

10:00

11:00

12:00

1:00

2:00

3:00

4:00

5:00

6:00

7:00

8:00

TO DO LIST

○
○
○
○
○
○
○
○

I plan to be more organised... tomorrow

NOTES

Daily Planner

/ /

SCHEDULE

6:00

7:00

8:00

9:00

10:00

11:00

12:00

1:00

2:00

3:00

4:00

5:00

6:00

7:00

8:00

TO DO LIST

○
○
○
○
○
○
○
○
○
○

I LOVE ME

NOTES

Daily Planner

SCHEDULE

6:00

7:00

8:00

9:00

10:00

11:00

12:00

1:00

2:00

3:00

4:00

5:00

6:00

7:00

8:00

TO DO LIST

◯

◯

◯

◯

◯

◯

◯

◯

Time to make things happen.

NOTES

Daily Planner

SCHEDULE

6:00

7:00

8:00

9:00

10:00

11:00

12:00

1:00

2:00

3:00

4:00

5:00

6:00

7:00

8:00

TO DO LIST

○
○
○
○
○
○
○
○

Wake up and chase your dreams.

NOTES

Daily Planner

SCHEDULE

6:00

7:00

8:00

9:00

10:00

11:00

12:00

1:00

2:00

3:00

4:00

5:00

6:00

7:00

8:00

TO DO LIST

○
○
○
○
○
○
○
○

I'm not weird, I'm just Limited Edition.

NOTES

Daily Planner

SCHEDULE

6:00

7:00

8:00

9:00

10:00

11:00

12:00

1:00

2:00

3:00

4:00

5:00

6:00

7:00

8:00

TO DO LIST

○
○
○
○
○
○
○
○

Mornings are tough, but so are you!

NOTES

Daily Planner

SCHEDULE

6:00

7:00

8:00

9:00

10:00

11:00

12:00

1:00

2:00

3:00

4:00

5:00

6:00

7:00

8:00

TO DO LIST

○
○
○
○
○
○
○
○

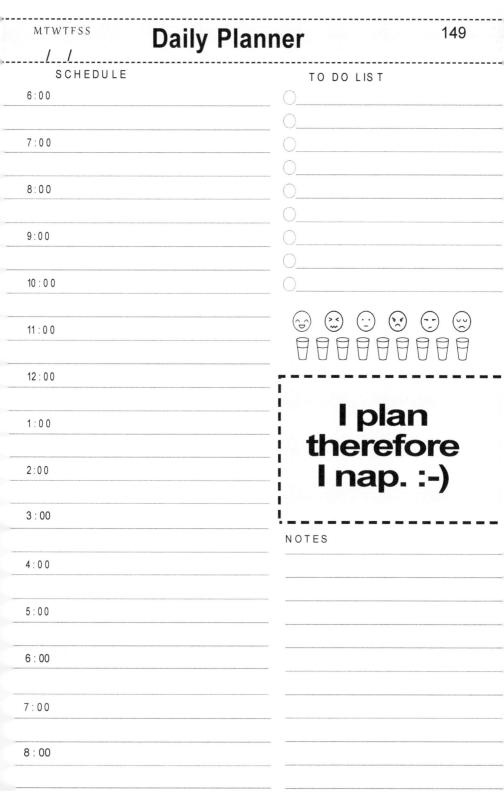

I plan therefore I nap. :-)

NOTES

Daily Planner

SCHEDULE

6:00

7:00

8:00

9:00

10:00

11:00

12:00

1:00

2:00

3:00

4:00

5:00

6:00

7:00

8:00

TO DO LIST

○
○
○
○
○
○
○
○

I'm not always right, but I'm never wrong. :-)

NOTES

Daily Planner

/ /

SCHEDULE

6:00

7:00

8:00

9:00

10:00

11:00

12:00

1:00

2:00

3:00

4:00

5:00

6:00

7:00

8:00

TO DO LIST

○
○
○
○
○
○
○
○

Visualize success. Imagine how good it will feel to finish.

NOTES

Daily Planner

SCHEDULE

6:00

7:00

8:00

9:00

10:00

11:00

12:00

1:00

2:00

3:00

4:00

5:00

6:00

7:00

8:00

TO DO LIST

○
○
○
○
○
○
○
○

Often & small breaks are the key to Big Success. ;-)

NOTES

MTWTFSS

Daily Planner

/ /

SCHEDULE

6:00

7:00

8:00

9:00

10:00

11:00

12:00

1:00

2:00

3:00

4:00

5:00

6:00

7:00

8:00

TO DO LIST

○
○
○
○
○
○
○
○

DO YOUR BEST

NOTES

Daily Planner

SCHEDULE

6:00

7:00

8:00

9:00

10:00

11:00

12:00

1:00

2:00

3:00

4:00

5:00

6:00

7:00

8:00

TO DO LIST

○

○

○

○

○

○

○

○

Eat.
Plan.
Sleep.
Repeat.

NOTES

/ /

Daily Planner

SCHEDULE

6:00

7:00

8:00

9:00

10:00

11:00

12:00

1:00

2:00

3:00

4:00

5:00

6:00

7:00

8:00

TO DO LIST

- ◯
- ◯
- ◯
- ◯
- ◯
- ◯
- ◯
- ◯

**Make work
a game
to conquer.**

NOTES

Daily Planner

SCHEDULE

6:00

7:00

8:00

9:00

10:00

11:00

12:00

1:00

2:00

3:00

4:00

5:00

6:00

7:00

8:00

TO DO LIST

○ _____
○ _____
○ _____
○ _____
○ _____
○ _____
○ _____
○ _____
○ _____
○ _____

Laugh often, it's the best medicine.

NOTES

Daily Planner

SCHEDULE

6:00

7:00

8:00

9:00

10:00

11:00

12:00

1:00

2:00

3:00

4:00

5:00

6:00

7:00

8:00

TO DO LIST

○
○
○
○
○
○
○
○

IF ALL ELSE
fails
TAKE A
~ nap ~

NOTES

Daily Planner

SCHEDULE

6:00

7:00

8:00

9:00

10:00

11:00

12:00

1:00

2:00

3:00

4:00

5:00

6:00

7:00

8:00

TO DO LIST

○
○
○
○
○
○
○
○
○

"Time may be a great healer, but it's a lousy beautician."

- Dorothy Parker

NOTES

Daily Planner

SCHEDULE

6:00

7:00

8:00

9:00

10:00

11:00

12:00

1:00

2:00

3:00

4:00

5:00

6:00

7:00

8:00

TO DO LIST

○
○
○
○
○
○
○
○

Life is too short to wait for tomorrow.

NOTES

Daily Planner

SCHEDULE

6:00

7:00

8:00

9:00

10:00

11:00

12:00

1:00

2:00

3:00

4:00

5:00

6:00

7:00

8:00

TO DO LIST

○
○
○
○
○
○
○
○

What do you call an alligator wearing a vest? An investigator. :-)

NOTES

Daily Planner

SCHEDULE

6:00

7:00

8:00

9:00

10:00

11:00

12:00

1:00

2:00

3:00

4:00

5:00

6:00

7:00

8:00

TO DO LIST

○
○
○
○
○
○
○
○

**Success =
Luck +
Pretending to know.
:-)**

NOTES

Daily Planner

SCHEDULE

6:00

7:00

8:00

9:00

10:00

11:00

12:00

1:00

2:00

3:00

4:00

5:00

6:00

7:00

8:00

TO DO LIST

○
○
○
○
○
○
○
○

Smile Breathe and Go Slowly

NOTES

Daily Planner

SCHEDULE

6:00

7:00

8:00

9:00

10:00

11:00

12:00

1:00

2:00

3:00

4:00

5:00

6:00

7:00

8:00

TO DO LIST

○

○

○

○

○

○

○

○

You're doing better than you think!

NOTES

Daily Planner

SCHEDULE

6:00

7:00

8:00

9:00

10:00

11:00

12:00

1:00

2:00

3:00

4:00

5:00

6:00

7:00

8:00

TO DO LIST

○
○
○
○
○
○
○
○
○
○

I'm not perfect, but my pet thinks I am.

NOTES

Daily Planner

SCHEDULE

6:00

7:00

8:00

9:00

10:00

11:00

12:00

1:00

2:00

3:00

4:00

5:00

6:00

7:00

8:00

TO DO LIST

○ _____

○ _____

○ _____

○ _____

○ _____

○ _____

○ _____

○ _____

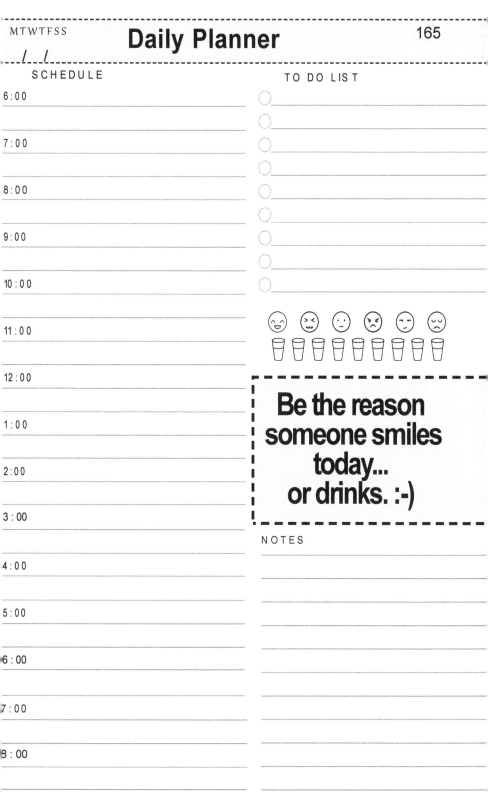

Be the reason someone smiles today... or drinks. :-)

NOTES

Daily Planner

SCHEDULE

6:00

7:00

8:00

9:00

10:00

11:00

12:00

1:00

2:00

3:00

4:00

5:00

6:00

7:00

8:00

TO DO LIST

○

○

○

○

○

○

○

○

LOVE your self FIRST

NOTES

Daily Planner

SCHEDULE

6:00

7:00

8:00

9:00

10:00

11:00

12:00

1:00

2:00

3:00

4:00

5:00

6:00

7:00

8:00

TO DO LIST

○

○

○

○

○

○

○

○

I'm just Fun-sized and Fabulous.

NOTES

Daily Planner

SCHEDULE

6:00

7:00

8:00

9:00

10:00

11:00

12:00

1:00

2:00

3:00

4:00

5:00

6:00

7:00

8:00

TO DO LIST

- ◯
- ◯
- ◯
- ◯
- ◯
- ◯
- ◯
- ◯
- ◯

"Whoever is happy
will make others
happy too."

-Anne Frank

NOTES

Daily Planner

SCHEDULE

6:00

7:00

8:00

9:00

10:00

11:00

12:00

1:00

2:00

3:00

4:00

5:00

6:00

7:00

8:00

TO DO LIST

○

○

○

○

○

○

○

○

"Life itself is the most wonderful fairy tale."

-Hans Christian Andersen

NOTES

Daily Planner

SCHEDULE

6:00

7:00

8:00

9:00

10:00

11:00

12:00

1:00

2:00

3:00

4:00

5:00

6:00

7:00

8:00

TO DO LIST

○
○
○
○
○
○
○
○

NOTES

Daily Planner

SCHEDULE

6:00

7:00

8:00

9:00

10:00

11:00

12:00

1:00

2:00

3:00

4:00

5:00

6:00

7:00

8:00

TO DO LIST

○
○
○
○
○
○
○
○

"No pressure, No diamonds."

- Thomas Carlyle

NOTES

Daily Planner

SCHEDULE

6:00

7:00

8:00

9:00

10:00

11:00

12:00

1:00

2:00

3:00

4:00

5:00

6:00

7:00

8:00

TO DO LIST

○

○

○

○

○

○

○

○

"Life is ours to be spent, not to be saved."

-D. H. Lawrence

NOTES

Daily Planner

SCHEDULE

6:00

7:00

8:00

9:00

10:00

11:00

12:00

1:00

2:00

3:00

4:00

5:00

6:00

7:00

8:00

TO DO LIST

- ◯ _____
- ◯ _____
- ◯ _____
- ◯ _____
- ◯ _____
- ◯ _____
- ◯ _____
- ◯ _____

Start

somewhere...

NOTES

Daily Planner

SCHEDULE

6:00

7:00

8:00

9:00

10:00

11:00

12:00

1:00

2:00

3:00

4:00

5:00

6:00

7:00

8:00

TO DO LIST

○
○
○
○
○
○
○
○
○

LOVE YOURSELF

NOTES

Daily Planner

/ /

SCHEDULE

6:00

7:00

8:00

9:00

10:00

11:00

12:00

1:00

2:00

3:00

4:00

5:00

6:00

7:00

8:00

TO DO LIST

○

○

○

○

○

○

○

○

"Don't let yesterday take too much of today."

- Will Rogers

NOTES

Daily Planner

MTWTFSS

/ /

SCHEDULE

6:00

7:00

8:00

9:00

10:00

11:00

12:00

1:00

2:00

3:00

4:00

5:00

6:00

7:00

8:00

TO DO LIST

○
○
○
○
○
○
○
○
○

Today
is the
Beginning.

NOTES

Daily Planner

SCHEDULE

6:00

7:00

8:00

9:00

10:00

11:00

12:00

1:00

2:00

3:00

4:00

5:00

6:00

7:00

8:00

TO DO LIST

- ○
- ○
- ○
- ○
- ○
- ○
- ○
- ○

"When nothing goes Right, go Left."

- Martha Cecilia

NOTES

Daily Planner

SCHEDULE

6:00

7:00

8:00

9:00

10:00

11:00

12:00

1:00

2:00

3:00

4:00

5:00

6:00

7:00

8:00

TO DO LIST

◯ _____
◯ _____
◯ _____
◯ _____
◯ _____
◯ _____
◯ _____
◯ _____
◯ _____
◯ _____

Don't stop until you're proud!

NOTES

Daily Planner

SCHEDULE

6:00

7:00

8:00

9:00

10:00

11:00

12:00

1:00

2:00

3:00

4:00

5:00

6:00

7:00

8:00

TO DO LIST

○
○
○
○
○
○
○
○

"Failure is Success in progress."

- Albert Einstein

NOTES

Daily Planner

SCHEDULE

6:00

7:00

8:00

9:00

10:00

11:00

12:00

1:00

2:00

3:00

4:00

5:00

6:00

7:00

8:00

TO DO LIST

○

○

○

○

○

○

○

○

○

Positive mind. Positive vibes. Positive life.

NOTES

Daily Planner

/__/

SCHEDULE

6:00

7:00

8:00

9:00

10:00

11:00

12:00

1:00

2:00

3:00

4:00

5:00

6:00

7:00

8:00

TO DO LIST

○
○
○
○
○
○
○
○

Learn to rest Not to quit.

- Banksy

NOTES

Daily Planner

SCHEDULE

6:00

7:00

8:00

9:00

10:00

11:00

12:00

1:00

2:00

3:00

4:00

5:00

6:00

7:00

8:00

TO DO LIST

○_____
○_____
○_____
○_____
○_____
○_____
○_____
○_____

😊 😖 😐 😠 😒 😟

DO YOUR THING

NOTES

Daily Planner

SCHEDULE

6:00

7:00

8:00

9:00

10:00

11:00

12:00

1:00

2:00

3:00

4:00

5:00

6:00

7:00

8:00

TO DO LIST

○
○
○
○
○
○
○
○

"If you think you can
you can,
if you think you can't
you're right!"
— Abraham Lincoln

NOTES

Daily Planner

SCHEDULE

6:00

7:00

8:00

9:00

10:00

11:00

12:00

1:00

2:00

3:00

4:00

5:00

6:00

7:00

8:00

TO DO LIST

○ _____
○ _____
○ _____
○ _____
○ _____
○ _____
○ _____
○ _____

DO IT YOUR SELF FOR

NOTES

Daily Planner

SCHEDULE

6:00

7:00

8:00

9:00

10:00

11:00

12:00

1:00

2:00

3:00

4:00

5:00

6:00

7:00

8:00

TO DO LIST

○
○
○
○
○
○
○
○

The way to get started is to quit talking and begin doing.

-Walt Disney

NOTES

Weekly Planner

MONDAY

TUESDAY

"You can destroy your now by worrying about tomorrow"

— Janis Joplin

WEDNESDAY

THURSDAY

FRIDAY

SATURDAY

"Success is not final, failure is not fatal:
it is the courage to continue that counts."

– Winston Churchill

SUNDAY

HABITS

	M	T	W	T	F	S	S
	☐	☐	☐	☐	☐	☐	☐
	☐	☐	☐	☐	☐	☐	☐
	☐	☐	☐	☐	☐	☐	☐
	☐	☐	☐	☐	☐	☐	☐
	☐	☐	☐	☐	☐	☐	☐
	☐	☐	☐	☐	☐	☐	☐
	☐	☐	☐	☐	☐	☐	☐
	☐	☐	☐	☐	☐	☐	☐
	☐	☐	☐	☐	☐	☐	☐
	☐	☐	☐	☐	☐	☐	☐

Weekly Planner

MONDAY

TUESDAY

"You don't have to be great to start, but you have to start to be great."
– Zig Ziglar

WEDNESDAY

THURSDAY

Weekly Planner

/ /

FRIDAY

_____
_____
_____
_____
_____
_____
_____
_____
_____
_____
_____
_____

SATURDAY

_____
_____
_____
_____
_____
_____
_____
_____
_____
_____
_____
_____

> *"The future belongs to those who believe in the beauty of their dreams."*
>
> *- Eleanor Roosevelt*

SUNDAY

_____
_____
_____
_____
_____
_____
_____
_____
_____
_____

HABITS

M	T	W	T	F	S	S
☐	☐	☐	☐	☐	☐	☐
☐	☐	☐	☐	☐	☐	☐
☐	☐	☐	☐	☐	☐	☐
☐	☐	☐	☐	☐	☐	☐
☐	☐	☐	☐	☐	☐	☐
☐	☐	☐	☐	☐	☐	☐
☐	☐	☐	☐	☐	☐	☐
☐	☐	☐	☐	☐	☐	☐
☐	☐	☐	☐	☐	☐	☐
☐	☐	☐	☐	☐	☐	☐

Weekly Planner

MONDAY

TUESDAY

"When you are inspired by some great purpose, all your thoughts break their bonds."

Patanjali

WEDNESDAY

THURSDAY

Weekly Planner

FRIDAY

SATURDAY

"Two things are infinite:
the Universe and human stupidity;
and I'm not sure about the Universe."

- Albert Einstein

SUNDAY

HABITS

M T W T F S S

Weekly Planner

MONDAY

_____
_____
_____
_____
_____
_____
_____
_____
_____
_____
_____

TUESDAY

_____
_____
_____
_____
_____
_____
_____
_____
_____
_____
_____

> "I've found that there is always some beauty left
> -- in nature, sunshine, freedom, in yourself;
> these can all help you."
> - Anne Frank

WEDNESDAY

_____
_____
_____
_____
_____
_____
_____
_____
_____
_____

THURSDAY

_____
_____
_____
_____
_____
_____
_____
_____
_____
_____

Weekly Planner

FRIDAY

SATURDAY

> "Things may come to those who wait,
>
> but only the things left by those who hustle."
>
> - Abraham Lincoln

SUNDAY

HABITS

M	T	W	T	F	S	S
☐	☐	☐	☐	☐	☐	☐
☐	☐	☐	☐	☐	☐	☐
☐	☐	☐	☐	☐	☐	☐
☐	☐	☐	☐	☐	☐	☐
☐	☐	☐	☐	☐	☐	☐
☐	☐	☐	☐	☐	☐	☐
☐	☐	☐	☐	☐	☐	☐
☐	☐	☐	☐	☐	☐	☐
☐	☐	☐	☐	☐	☐	☐
☐	☐	☐	☐	☐	☐	☐

Weekly Planner

MONDAY

TUESDAY

*"Don't watch the clock;
do what it does. Keep going."*
- Sam Levenson

WEDNESDAY

THURSDAY

Weekly Planner

/ /

FRIDAY

_____
_____
_____
_____
_____
_____
_____
_____
_____
_____
_____
_____

SATURDAY

_____
_____
_____
_____
_____
_____
_____
_____
_____
_____
_____
_____

"Nothing is permanent in this wicked world
- not even our troubles."

- Charlie Chaplin

SUNDAY

_____
_____
_____
_____
_____
_____
_____
_____
_____
_____

HABITS

	M	T	W	T	F	S	S
	☐	☐	☐	☐	☐	☐	☐
	☐	☐	☐	☐	☐	☐	☐
	☐	☐	☐	☐	☐	☐	☐
	☐	☐	☐	☐	☐	☐	☐
	☐	☐	☐	☐	☐	☐	☐
	☐	☐	☐	☐	☐	☐	☐
	☐	☐	☐	☐	☐	☐	☐
	☐	☐	☐	☐	☐	☐	☐
	☐	☐	☐	☐	☐	☐	☐
	☐	☐	☐	☐	☐	☐	☐

Weekly Planner

MONDAY

TUESDAY

"Do not go where the path may lead,
go instead where there is no path and leave a trail."

-Ralph Waldo Emerson

WEDNESDAY

THURSDAY

Weekly Planner

FRIDAY

_____
_____
_____
_____
_____
_____
_____
_____
_____
_____
_____

SATURDAY

_____
_____
_____
_____
_____
_____
_____
_____
_____
_____
_____

Many of life's failures are people who did not realize how close they were to success when they gave up.

-Thomas A. Edison

SUNDAY

_____
_____
_____
_____
_____
_____
_____
_____
_____
_____

HABITS

M	T	W	T	F	S	S
☐	☐	☐	☐	☐	☐	☐
☐	☐	☐	☐	☐	☐	☐
☐	☐	☐	☐	☐	☐	☐
☐	☐	☐	☐	☐	☐	☐
☐	☐	☐	☐	☐	☐	☐
☐	☐	☐	☐	☐	☐	☐
☐	☐	☐	☐	☐	☐	☐
☐	☐	☐	☐	☐	☐	☐
☐	☐	☐	☐	☐	☐	☐
☐	☐	☐	☐	☐	☐	☐

Weekly Planner

MONDAY

TUESDAY

---

*"Success is not the key to happiness.
Happiness is the key to success.
If you love what you are doing,
you will be successful."* – Albert Schweitzer

WEDNESDAY

THURSDAY

FRIDAY

SATURDAY

"The only time success comes before work
is in the dictionary." (and in the coffee shop).
- Vince Lombardi

SUNDAY

HABITS

	M	T	W	T	F	S	S
	☐	☐	☐	☐	☐	☐	☐
	☐	☐	☐	☐	☐	☐	☐
	☐	☐	☐	☐	☐	☐	☐
	☐	☐	☐	☐	☐	☐	☐
	☐	☐	☐	☐	☐	☐	☐
	☐	☐	☐	☐	☐	☐	☐
	☐	☐	☐	☐	☐	☐	☐
	☐	☐	☐	☐	☐	☐	☐
	☐	☐	☐	☐	☐	☐	☐
	☐	☐	☐	☐	☐	☐	☐

Weekly Planner

MONDAY

TUESDAY

"The only person you are destined to become is the person you decide to be."

– Ralph Waldo Emerson

WEDNESDAY

THURSDAY

FRIDAY

SATURDAY

"Don't stop when you're tired.
Stop when you're done." - Marilyn Monroe

SUNDAY

HABITS

M	T	W	T	F	S	S
☐	☐	☐	☐	☐	☐	☐
☐	☐	☐	☐	☐	☐	☐
☐	☐	☐	☐	☐	☐	☐
☐	☐	☐	☐	☐	☐	☐
☐	☐	☐	☐	☐	☐	☐
☐	☐	☐	☐	☐	☐	☐
☐	☐	☐	☐	☐	☐	☐
☐	☐	☐	☐	☐	☐	☐
☐	☐	☐	☐	☐	☐	☐
☐	☐	☐	☐	☐	☐	☐

Weekly Planner

MONDAY

_____
_____
_____
_____
_____
_____
_____
_____
_____
_____
_____

TUESDAY

_____
_____
_____
_____
_____
_____
_____
_____
_____
_____
_____

"The moment you realize your worth is the moment you stop settling for less than you deserve." - Unknown

WEDNESDAY

_____
_____
_____
_____
_____
_____
_____
_____
_____

THURSDAY

_____
_____
_____
_____
_____
_____
_____
_____
_____

Weekly Planner

FRIDAY

SATURDAY

"Go confidently in the direction of your dreams!
Live the life you've imagined."

-Henry David Thoreau

SUNDAY

HABITS

M T W T F S S

Weekly Planner

MONDAY

TUESDAY

---

*"In three words I can sum up everything
I've learned about life: it goes on."*

-Robert Frost

WEDNESDAY

THURSDAY

FRIDAY

_____
_____
_____
_____
_____
_____
_____
_____
_____
_____
_____

SATURDAY

_____
_____
_____
_____
_____
_____
_____
_____
_____
_____
_____

"It does not matter how slowly you go as long as you do not stop." - Confucius

SUNDAY

_____
_____
_____
_____
_____
_____
_____
_____
_____
_____
_____

HABITS

M T W T F S S
☐ ☐ ☐ ☐ ☐ ☐ ☐
☐ ☐ ☐ ☐ ☐ ☐ ☐
☐ ☐ ☐ ☐ ☐ ☐ ☐
☐ ☐ ☐ ☐ ☐ ☐ ☐
☐ ☐ ☐ ☐ ☐ ☐ ☐
☐ ☐ ☐ ☐ ☐ ☐ ☐
☐ ☐ ☐ ☐ ☐ ☐ ☐
☐ ☐ ☐ ☐ ☐ ☐ ☐
☐ ☐ ☐ ☐ ☐ ☐ ☐
☐ ☐ ☐ ☐ ☐ ☐ ☐

Weekly Planner

MONDAY

TUESDAY

*"If you want to live a happy life,
tie it to a goal, not to people or things."*
— Albert Einstein

WEDNESDAY

THURSDAY

FRIDAY

SATURDAY

> The secret of success is to do
> the common thing uncommonly well.
>
> -John D. Rockefeller Jr.

SUNDAY

HABITS

M T W T F S S

Weekly Planner

MONDAY

TUESDAY

"To love oneself is the beginning of a lifelong romance." - Oscar Wilde

WEDNESDAY

THURSDAY

FRIDAY

SATURDAY

"You don't have to be perfect to be amazing."

- Unknown

SUNDAY

HABITS

	M	T	W	T	F	S	S
	☐	☐	☐	☐	☐	☐	☐
	☐	☐	☐	☐	☐	☐	☐
	☐	☐	☐	☐	☐	☐	☐
	☐	☐	☐	☐	☐	☐	☐
	☐	☐	☐	☐	☐	☐	☐
	☐	☐	☐	☐	☐	☐	☐
	☐	☐	☐	☐	☐	☐	☐
	☐	☐	☐	☐	☐	☐	☐
	☐	☐	☐	☐	☐	☐	☐
	☐	☐	☐	☐	☐	☐	☐

Weekly Planner

MONDAY

TUESDAY

"A goal without a plan is just a wish."

– Antoine de Saint-Exupéry

WEDNESDAY

THURSDAY

Weekly Planner

/ /

FRIDAY

SATURDAY

"*Success is not final; failure is not fatal:
It is the courage to continue that counts.*"

-Winston S. Churchill

SUNDAY

HABITS

M T W T F S S

Weekly Planner

MONDAY

TUESDAY

"The most important thing in life is to stop saying 'I wish' and start saying 'I will'."

— Charles Dickens

WEDNESDAY

THURSDAY

Weekly Planner

FRIDAY

SATURDAY

"I don't need a hairstylist, my pillow gives me a new hairstyle every morning."

-Unknown

SUNDAY

HABITS

	M	T	W	T	F	S	S
	☐	☐	☐	☐	☐	☐	☐
	☐	☐	☐	☐	☐	☐	☐
	☐	☐	☐	☐	☐	☐	☐
	☐	☐	☐	☐	☐	☐	☐
	☐	☐	☐	☐	☐	☐	☐
	☐	☐	☐	☐	☐	☐	☐
	☐	☐	☐	☐	☐	☐	☐
	☐	☐	☐	☐	☐	☐	☐
	☐	☐	☐	☐	☐	☐	☐
	☐	☐	☐	☐	☐	☐	☐

Weekly Planner

MONDAY

TUESDAY

"Twenty years from now you will be more disappointed by the things that you didn't do than by the ones you did do."

- Mark Twain

WEDNESDAY

THURSDAY

Weekly Planner

FRIDAY

SATURDAY

*"I don't always follow the rules,
but when I do, it's because I made them."*

:-) - Unknown

SUNDAY

HABITS

	M	T	W	T	F	S	S
	☐	☐	☐	☐	☐	☐	☐
	☐	☐	☐	☐	☐	☐	☐
	☐	☐	☐	☐	☐	☐	☐
	☐	☐	☐	☐	☐	☐	☐
	☐	☐	☐	☐	☐	☐	☐
	☐	☐	☐	☐	☐	☐	☐
	☐	☐	☐	☐	☐	☐	☐
	☐	☐	☐	☐	☐	☐	☐
	☐	☐	☐	☐	☐	☐	☐
	☐	☐	☐	☐	☐	☐	☐

Weekly Planner

MONDAY

TUESDAY

"We are what we repeatedly do; excellence, then, is not an act but a habit."

- Aristotle

WEDNESDAY

THURSDAY

Weekly Planner

FRIDAY

SATURDAY

"Be proud of who you are, and not ashamed of how someone else sees you."

- Unknown

SUNDAY

HABITS

M	T	W	T	F	S	S
☐	☐	☐	☐	☐	☐	☐
☐	☐	☐	☐	☐	☐	☐
☐	☐	☐	☐	☐	☐	☐
☐	☐	☐	☐	☐	☐	☐
☐	☐	☐	☐	☐	☐	☐
☐	☐	☐	☐	☐	☐	☐
☐	☐	☐	☐	☐	☐	☐
☐	☐	☐	☐	☐	☐	☐
☐	☐	☐	☐	☐	☐	☐
☐	☐	☐	☐	☐	☐	☐

Weekly Planner

MONDAY

TUESDAY

"Without goals, and plans to reach them, you are like a ship that has set sail with no destination."

- Fitzhugh Dodson

WEDNESDAY

THURSDAY

Weekly Planner

FRIDAY

SATURDAY

"I never make the same mistake twice.
I make it like five or six times,
you know, just to be sure." - Unknown

SUNDAY

HABITS

M T W T F S S

Weekly Planner

MONDAY

TUESDAY

Physical exercise and taking care of your body can contribute to your happiness and overall well-being.

WEDNESDAY

THURSDAY

MTWTFSS
/ /
Weekly Planner 221

FRIDAY   SATURDAY

Planning can help you to develop a more
positive mindset, as you focus on what
you can achieve rather than what you can't.

SUNDAY   HABITS

M T W T F S S

Weekly Planner

MONDAY

TUESDAY

---

*Smiling is contagious
and can uplift the mood of those
around you.*

WEDNESDAY

THURSDAY

FRIDAY

SATURDAY

*"I'm not always late,
I'm just on a different time zone." :-)*

SUNDAY

HABITS

M	T	W	T	F	S	S
☐	☐	☐	☐	☐	☐	☐
☐	☐	☐	☐	☐	☐	☐
☐	☐	☐	☐	☐	☐	☐
☐	☐	☐	☐	☐	☐	☐
☐	☐	☐	☐	☐	☐	☐
☐	☐	☐	☐	☐	☐	☐
☐	☐	☐	☐	☐	☐	☐
☐	☐	☐	☐	☐	☐	☐
☐	☐	☐	☐	☐	☐	☐
☐	☐	☐	☐	☐	☐	☐

Weekly Planner

MONDAY

TUESDAY

---

*"The pessimist sees difficulty in every opportunity.
The optimist sees the opportunity
in every difficulty."*

- Winston Churchill

WEDNESDAY

THURSDAY

Weekly Planner

FRIDAY

SATURDAY

A positive mindset attracts positive results.

SUNDAY

HABITS

	M	T	W	T	F	S	S
	☐	☐	☐	☐	☐	☐	☐
	☐	☐	☐	☐	☐	☐	☐
	☐	☐	☐	☐	☐	☐	☐
	☐	☐	☐	☐	☐	☐	☐
	☐	☐	☐	☐	☐	☐	☐
	☐	☐	☐	☐	☐	☐	☐
	☐	☐	☐	☐	☐	☐	☐
	☐	☐	☐	☐	☐	☐	☐
	☐	☐	☐	☐	☐	☐	☐
	☐	☐	☐	☐	☐	☐	☐

Weekly Planner

MONDAY

TUESDAY

---

*"The question isn't who is going to let me;
it's who is going to stop me."*

- Ayn Rand

WEDNESDAY

THURSDAY

FRIDAY

_____
_____
_____
_____
_____
_____
_____
_____
_____
_____
_____
_____

SATURDAY

_____
_____
_____
_____
_____
_____
_____
_____
_____
_____
_____

Mindfulness can be practiced through meditation or simply by being aware of your surroundings.

SUNDAY

_____
_____
_____
_____
_____
_____
_____
_____
_____
_____
_____
_____

HABITS

	M	T	W	T	F	S	S
	☐	☐	☐	☐	☐	☐	☐
	☐	☐	☐	☐	☐	☐	☐
	☐	☐	☐	☐	☐	☐	☐
	☐	☐	☐	☐	☐	☐	☐
	☐	☐	☐	☐	☐	☐	☐
	☐	☐	☐	☐	☐	☐	☐
	☐	☐	☐	☐	☐	☐	☐
	☐	☐	☐	☐	☐	☐	☐
	☐	☐	☐	☐	☐	☐	☐
	☐	☐	☐	☐	☐	☐	☐

Weekly Planner

MONDAY

TUESDAY

"Challenges are what make life interesting and overcoming them is what makes life meaningful."

- Joshua J. Marine

WEDNESDAY

THURSDAY

FRIDAY

_____
_____
_____
_____
_____
_____
_____
_____
_____
_____
_____

SATURDAY

_____
_____
_____
_____
_____
_____
_____
_____
_____
_____
_____

> *"Always remember that you are*
> *absolutely unique.*
> *Just like everyone else."*
>
> *- Margaret Meade*

SUNDAY

_____
_____
_____
_____
_____
_____
_____
_____
_____
_____

HABITS

M	T	W	T	F	S	S
☐	☐	☐	☐	☐	☐	☐
☐	☐	☐	☐	☐	☐	☐
☐	☐	☐	☐	☐	☐	☐
☐	☐	☐	☐	☐	☐	☐
☐	☐	☐	☐	☐	☐	☐
☐	☐	☐	☐	☐	☐	☐
☐	☐	☐	☐	☐	☐	☐
☐	☐	☐	☐	☐	☐	☐
☐	☐	☐	☐	☐	☐	☐
☐	☐	☐	☐	☐	☐	☐

Weekly Planner

MONDAY

_____
_____
_____
_____
_____
_____
_____
_____
_____
_____
_____

TUESDAY

_____
_____
_____
_____
_____
_____
_____
_____
_____
_____
_____

> "Sing like no one's listening,
> love like you've never been hurt,
> dance like nobody's watching,
> and live like it's heaven on Earth."
> – Mark Twain

WEDNESDAY

_____
_____
_____
_____
_____
_____
_____
_____
_____
_____

THURSDAY

_____
_____
_____
_____
_____
_____
_____
_____
_____
_____

Weekly Planner

FRIDAY

_____
_____
_____
_____
_____
_____
_____
_____
_____
_____
_____
_____

SATURDAY

_____
_____
_____
_____
_____
_____
_____
_____
_____
_____
_____

*Success is living the life as you want it,
not as someone else.*

- Mirela S Tipping

SUNDAY

_____
_____
_____
_____
_____
_____
_____
_____
_____
_____

HABITS

M	T	W	T	F	S	S
☐	☐	☐	☐	☐	☐	☐
☐	☐	☐	☐	☐	☐	☐
☐	☐	☐	☐	☐	☐	☐
☐	☐	☐	☐	☐	☐	☐
☐	☐	☐	☐	☐	☐	☐
☐	☐	☐	☐	☐	☐	☐
☐	☐	☐	☐	☐	☐	☐
☐	☐	☐	☐	☐	☐	☐
☐	☐	☐	☐	☐	☐	☐
☐	☐	☐	☐	☐	☐	☐

Weekly Planner

MONDAY

TUESDAY

"The best and most beautiful things in this world cannot be seen or even heard, but must be felt with the heart."

- Helen Keller

WEDNESDAY

THURSDAY

FRIDAY

_____
_____
_____
_____
_____
_____
_____
_____
_____
_____
_____
_____

SATURDAY

_____
_____
_____
_____
_____
_____
_____
_____
_____
_____
_____
_____

"To be brave is to love someone unconditionally, without expecting anything in return."

- Margaret Mitchell

Start with loving yourself...

SUNDAY

_____
_____
_____
_____
_____
_____
_____
_____
_____
_____
_____

HABITS

M T W T F S S

☐☐☐☐☐☐☐
☐☐☐☐☐☐☐
☐☐☐☐☐☐☐
☐☐☐☐☐☐☐
☐☐☐☐☐☐☐
☐☐☐☐☐☐☐
☐☐☐☐☐☐☐
☐☐☐☐☐☐☐
☐☐☐☐☐☐☐
☐☐☐☐☐☐☐

Weekly Planner

MONDAY

TUESDAY

"You can destroy your now by worrying about tomorrow"

— Janis Joplin

WEDNESDAY

THURSDAY

Weekly Planner

FRIDAY

_____
_____
_____
_____
_____
_____
_____
_____
_____
_____
_____
_____

SATURDAY

_____
_____
_____
_____
_____
_____
_____
_____
_____
_____
_____
_____

"Success is not final, failure is not fatal:
it is the courage to continue that counts."
- Winston Churchill

SUNDAY

_____
_____
_____
_____
_____
_____
_____
_____
_____

HABITS

M	T	W	T	F	S	S
☐	☐	☐	☐	☐	☐	☐
☐	☐	☐	☐	☐	☐	☐
☐	☐	☐	☐	☐	☐	☐
☐	☐	☐	☐	☐	☐	☐
☐	☐	☐	☐	☐	☐	☐
☐	☐	☐	☐	☐	☐	☐
☐	☐	☐	☐	☐	☐	☐
☐	☐	☐	☐	☐	☐	☐
☐	☐	☐	☐	☐	☐	☐
☐	☐	☐	☐	☐	☐	☐

Weekly Planner

MONDAY

TUESDAY

---

*"You don't have to be great to start,
but you have to start to be great."*
– Zig Ziglar

WEDNESDAY

THURSDAY

Weekly Planner

FRIDAY

SATURDAY

"The future belongs to those who believe in the beauty of their dreams."

- Eleanor Roosevelt

SUNDAY

HABITS

	M	T	W	T	F	S	S
	☐	☐	☐	☐	☐	☐	☐
	☐	☐	☐	☐	☐	☐	☐
	☐	☐	☐	☐	☐	☐	☐
	☐	☐	☐	☐	☐	☐	☐
	☐	☐	☐	☐	☐	☐	☐
	☐	☐	☐	☐	☐	☐	☐
	☐	☐	☐	☐	☐	☐	☐
	☐	☐	☐	☐	☐	☐	☐
	☐	☐	☐	☐	☐	☐	☐
	☐	☐	☐	☐	☐	☐	☐

MONTH:

Monday	Tuesday	Wednesday

YEAR:

Thursday	Friday	Saturday	Sunday

MONTH:

Monday	Tuesday	Wednesday

YEAR:

Thursday	Friday	Saturday	Sunday

MONTH:

Monday	Tuesday	Wednesday

YEAR:

Thursday	Friday	Saturday	Sunday

MONTH:

Monday	Tuesday	Wednesday

YEAR:

Thursday	Friday	Saturday	Sunday

MONTH:

Monday	Tuesday	Wednesday

YEAR:

Thursday	Friday	Saturday	Sunday

MONTH:

Monday	Tuesday	Wednesday

YEAR:

Thursday	Friday	Saturday	Sunday

MONTH:

Monday	Tuesday	Wednesday

YEAR:

Thursday	Friday	Saturday	Sunday

MONTH:

Monday	Tuesday	Wednesday

YEAR:

Thursday	Friday	Saturday	Sunday

MONTH:

Monday	Tuesday	Wednesday

YEAR:

Thursday	Friday	Saturday	Sunday

MONTH:

Monday	Tuesday	Wednesday

YEAR:

Thursday	Friday	Saturday	Sunday

MONTH:

Monday	Tuesday	Wednesday

YEAR:

Thursday	Friday	Saturday	Sunday

MONTH:

Monday	Tuesday	Wednesday

YEAR:

Thursday	Friday	Saturday	Sunday

YEAR

JANURAY

_____
_____
_____
_____
_____
_____
_____
_____

FEBRUARY

1 _____
2 _____
3 _____
4 _____
5 _____
6 _____
7 _____

MARCH

1 _____
2 _____
3 _____
4 _____
5 _____
6 _____
7 _____

APRIL

_____
_____
_____
_____
_____
_____
_____
_____

MAY

1 _____
2 _____
3 _____
4 _____
5 _____
6 _____
7 _____

JUNE

1 _____
2 _____
3 _____
4 _____
5 _____
6 _____
7 _____

JULY

_____
_____
_____
_____
_____
_____
_____
_____

AUGUST

1 _____
2 _____
3 _____
4 _____
5 _____
6 _____
7 _____

SEPTEMBER

1 _____
2 _____
3 _____
4 _____
5 _____
6 _____
7 _____

OCTOBER

_____
_____
_____
_____
_____
_____
_____
_____

NOVEMBER

1 _____
2 _____
3 _____
4 _____
5 _____
6 _____
7 _____

DECEMBER

1 _____
2 _____
3 _____
4 _____
5 _____
6 _____
7 _____

JANURAY

FEBRUARY

1
2
3
4
5
6
7

MARCH

1
2
3
4
5
6
7

APRIL

MAY

1
2
3
4
5
6
7

JUNE

1
2
3
4
5
6
7

JULY

AUGUST

1
2
3
4
5
6
7

SEPTEMBER

1
2
3
4
5
6
7

OCTOBER

NOVEMBER

1
2
3
4
5
6
7

DECEMBER

1
2
3
4
5
6
7

Gratitude & Journal Prompts:

Writing a gratitude log from time to time is like a warm and fuzzy blanket for your soul. It's a way to wrap yourself up in all the good things in your life and bask in their glow. It's like a reminder that no matter how tough things get, there's always something to be thankful for. Plus, it's a great way to shift your focus away from negative thoughts and emotions and to cultivate a more positive and grateful mindset.

These are some ideas of what you can write in the following pages. Add the chosen ones to your Content page, to make it easier to check on them later.

1. A challenge that helped me was...
2. I'm grateful I have enough money to be able to...
3. I'm grateful I am healthy enough to...
4. The thing I love about my friend is...
5. Something that makes me laugh is...
6. Something about me that I'd like to celebrate is...
7. What I'm excited about the most is...
8. Someone who helped me get where I am today is...
9. One reason my life is wonderful is...
10. Something that worked out better than I hoped is...
11. Someone who makes me happy is...
12. Something I get to do today that I've always wanted to do is...
13. One reason I am happy right now is that...
14. A valuable lesson I learnt is...
15. Things that make me smile are…
16. An unforgettable memory I have and treasure is...
17. I appreciate my family because...
18. The places I most appreciate are...
19. Things I wish to change about how I think…
20. Things I wish to change about how I feel…
21. My greatest strengths are…
22. Some things that make me happy are…
23. Things I love about me…

So, grab a cozy blanket, your favorite notebook,
and start snuggling up with your gratitude log today!

1. Someone that inspires / motivates me is … (because…)
2. Something I regretted not doing and what I would do different…
3. Ways I can show kindness to myself and others are…
4. Things that make me insecure are…
5. Ways that would help me change that thinking are…
6. Reasons I should not care about what other think about me…
7. Things I wish were different and how can I get them…
8. Something / Someone I am proud of…
9. Actions that I can do right now to improve…
10. Things that have been bothering me lately…
11. What does Happiness means to me?
12. Are my goals really what I want?
13. What stays between me and my dream life?
14. How can I simplify my life and focus on what is more important?
15. What habits make your life better and how?
16. Consider your ideal life. Make a note of it and how can you make it happen.
17. Bad Habits I need to stop…
18. What are your top five priorities in life?
19. Describe your ideal day.
20. What's something you'd like to change about yourself?
21. What's one thing you're looking forward to?
22. What's something you wish you had more time for?
23. Write about a time when you felt really motivated.
24. What's one thing you could do to improve your self-care routine?
25. Write a bucket list of things you want to do in your lifetime.
26. Write about a time when you failed and what you learned from it.
27. Describe your dream job.
28. What is your favorite hobby and why do you enjoy it?
29. Who is someone you admire and why?
30. What are some limiting beliefs you have, and how can you challenge them?
31. What are some things you've been hesitant to forgive, and why?
32. How can I show gratitude and appreciation for the people in my social circle?

2023 Calendar

January

Mo	Tu	We	Th	Fr	Sa	Su
						1
2	3	4	5	6	7	8
9	10	11	12	13	14	15
16	17	18	19	20	21	22
23	24	25	26	27	28	29
30	31					

February

Mo	Tu	We	Th	Fr	Sa	Su
		1	2	3	4	5
6	7	8	9	10	11	12
13	14	15	16	17	18	19
20	21	22	23	24	25	26
27	28					

March

Mo	Tu	We	Th	Fr	Sa	Su
		1	2	3	4	5
6	7	8	9	10	11	12
13	14	15	16	17	18	19
20	21	22	23	24	25	26
27	28	29	30	31		

April

Mo	Tu	We	Th	Fr	Sa	Su
					1	2
3	4	5	6	7	8	9
10	11	12	13	14	15	16
17	18	19	20	21	22	23
24	25	26	27	28	29	30

May

Mo	Tu	We	Th	Fr	Sa	Su
1	2	3	4	5	6	7
8	9	10	11	12	13	14
15	16	17	18	19	20	21
22	23	24	25	26	27	28
29	30	31				

June

Mo	Tu	We	Th	Fr	Sa	Su
			1	2	3	4
5	6	7	8	9	10	11
12	13	14	15	16	17	18
19	20	21	22	23	24	25
26	27	28	29	30		

July

Mo	Tu	We	Th	Fr	Sa	Su
					1	2
3	4	5	6	7	8	9
10	11	12	13	14	15	16
17	18	19	20	21	22	23
24	25	26	27	28	29	30
31						

August

Mo	Tu	We	Th	Fr	Sa	Su
	1	2	3	4	5	6
7	8	9	10	11	12	13
14	15	16	17	18	19	20
21	22	23	24	25	26	27
28	29	30	31			

September

Mo	Tu	We	Th	Fr	Sa	Su
				1	2	3
4	5	6	7	8	9	10
11	12	13	14	15	16	17
18	19	20	21	22	23	24
25	26	27	28	29	30	

October

Mo	Tu	We	Th	Fr	Sa	Su
						1
2	3	4	5	6	7	8
9	10	11	12	13	14	15
16	17	18	19	20	21	22
23	24	25	26	27	28	29
30	31					

November

Mo	Tu	We	Th	Fr	Sa	Su
		1	2	3	4	5
6	7	8	9	10	11	12
13	14	15	16	17	18	19
20	21	22	23	24	25	26
27	28	29	30			

December

Mo	Tu	We	Th	Fr	Sa	Su
				1	2	3
4	5	6	7	8	9	10
11	12	13	14	15	16	17
18	19	20	21	22	23	24
25	26	27	28	29	30	31

2024 Calendar

January

Mo	Tu	We	Th	Fr	Sa	Su
1	2	3	4	5	6	7
8	9	10	11	12	13	14
15	16	17	18	19	20	21
22	23	24	25	26	27	28
29	30	31				

February

Mo	Tu	We	Th	Fr	Sa	Su
			1	2	3	4
5	6	7	8	9	10	11
12	13	14	15	16	17	18
19	20	21	22	23	24	25
26	27	28	29			

March

Mo	Tu	We	Th	Fr	Sa	Su
				1	2	3
4	5	6	7	8	9	10
11	12	13	14	15	16	17
18	19	20	21	22	23	24
25	26	27	28	29	30	31

April

Mo	Tu	We	Th	Fr	Sa	Su
1	2	3	4	5	6	7
8	9	10	11	12	13	14
15	16	17	18	19	20	21
22	23	24	25	26	27	28
29	30					

May

Mo	Tu	We	Th	Fr	Sa	Su
		1	2	3	4	5
6	7	8	9	10	11	12
13	14	15	16	17	18	19
20	21	22	23	24	25	26
27	28	29	30	31		

June

Mo	Tu	We	Th	Fr	Sa	Su
					1	2
3	4	5	6	7	8	9
10	11	12	13	14	15	16
17	18	19	20	21	22	23
24	25	26	27	28	29	30

July

Mo	Tu	We	Th	Fr	Sa	Su
1	2	3	4	5	6	7
8	9	10	11	12	13	14
15	16	17	18	19	20	21
22	23	24	25	26	27	28
29	30	31				

August

Mo	Tu	We	Th	Fr	Sa	Su
			1	2	3	4
5	6	7	8	9	10	11
12	13	14	15	16	17	18
19	20	21	22	23	24	25
26	27	28	29	30	31	

September

Mo	Tu	We	Th	Fr	Sa	Su
						1
2	3	4	5	6	7	8
9	10	11	12	13	14	15
16	17	18	19	20	21	22
23	24	25	26	27	28	29
30						

October

Mo	Tu	We	Th	Fr	Sa	Su
	1	2	3	4	5	6
7	8	9	10	11	12	13
14	15	16	17	18	19	20
21	22	23	24	25	26	27
28	29	30	31			

November

Mo	Tu	We	Th	Fr	Sa	Su
				1	2	3
4	5	6	7	8	9	10
11	12	13	14	15	16	17
18	19	20	21	22	23	24
25	26	27	28	29	30	

December

Mo	Tu	We	Th	Fr	Sa	Su
						1
2	3	4	5	6	7	8
9	10	11	12	13	14	15
16	17	18	19	20	21	22
23	24	25	26	27	28	29
30	31					

2025 Calendar

January

Mo	Tu	We	Th	Fr	Sa	Su
		1	2	3	4	5
6	7	8	9	10	11	12
13	14	15	16	17	18	19
20	21	22	23	24	25	26
27	28	29	30	31		

February

Mo	Tu	We	Th	Fr	Sa	Su
					1	2
3	4	5	6	7	8	9
10	11	12	13	14	15	16
17	18	19	20	21	22	23
24	25	26	27	28		

March

Mo	Tu	We	Th	Fr	Sa	Su
					1	2
3	4	5	6	7	8	9
10	11	12	13	14	15	16
17	18	19	20	21	22	23
24	25	26	27	28	29	30
31						

April

Mo	Tu	We	Th	Fr	Sa	Su
	1	2	3	4	5	6
7	8	9	10	11	12	13
14	15	16	17	18	19	20
21	22	23	24	25	26	27
28	29	30				

May

Mo	Tu	We	Th	Fr	Sa	Su
			1	2	3	4
5	6	7	8	9	10	11
12	13	14	15	16	17	18
19	20	21	22	23	24	25
26	27	28	29	30	31	

June

Mo	Tu	We	Th	Fr	Sa	Su
						1
2	3	4	5	6	7	8
9	10	11	12	13	14	15
16	17	18	19	20	21	22
23	24	25	26	27	28	29
30						

July

Mo	Tu	We	Th	Fr	Sa	Su
	1	2	3	4	5	6
7	8	9	10	11	12	13
14	15	16	17	18	19	20
21	22	23	24	25	26	27
28	29	30	31			

August

Mo	Tu	We	Th	Fr	Sa	Su
				1	2	3
4	5	6	7	8	9	10
11	12	13	14	15	16	17
18	19	20	21	22	23	24
25	26	27	28	29	30	31

September

Mo	Tu	We	Th	Fr	Sa	Su
1	2	3	4	5	6	7
8	9	10	11	12	13	14
15	16	17	18	19	20	21
22	23	24	25	26	27	28
29	30					

October

Mo	Tu	We	Th	Fr	Sa	Su
		1	2	3	4	5
6	7	8	9	10	11	12
13	14	15	16	17	18	19
20	21	22	23	24	25	26
27	28	29	30	31		

November

Mo	Tu	We	Th	Fr	Sa	Su
					1	2
3	4	5	6	7	8	9
10	11	12	13	14	15	16
17	18	19	20	21	22	23
24	25	26	27	28	29	30

December

Mo	Tu	We	Th	Fr	Sa	Su
1	2	3	4	5	6	7
8	9	10	11	12	13	14
15	16	17	18	19	20	21
22	23	24	25	26	27	28
29	30	31				

2026 Calendar

January

Mo	Tu	We	Th	Fr	Sa	Su
			1	2	3	4
5	6	7	8	9	10	11
12	13	14	15	16	17	18
19	20	21	22	23	24	25
26	27	28	29	30	31	

February

Mo	Tu	We	Th	Fr	Sa	Su
						1
2	3	4	5	6	7	8
9	10	11	12	13	14	15
16	17	18	19	20	21	22
23	24	25	26	27	28	

March

Mo	Tu	We	Th	Fr	Sa	Su
						1
2	3	4	5	6	7	8
9	10	11	12	13	14	15
16	17	18	19	20	21	22
23	24	25	26	27	28	29
30	31					

April

Mo	Tu	We	Th	Fr	Sa	Su
		1	2	3	4	5
6	7	8	9	10	11	12
13	14	15	16	17	18	19
20	21	22	23	24	25	26
27	28	29	30			

May

Mo	Tu	We	Th	Fr	Sa	Su
				1	2	3
4	5	6	7	8	9	10
11	12	13	14	15	16	17
18	19	20	21	22	23	24
25	26	27	28	29	30	31

June

Mo	Tu	We	Th	Fr	Sa	Su
1	2	3	4	5	6	7
8	9	10	11	12	13	14
15	16	17	18	19	20	21
22	23	24	25	26	27	28
29	30					

July

Mo	Tu	We	Th	Fr	Sa	Su
		1	2	3	4	5
6	7	8	9	10	11	12
13	14	15	16	17	18	19
20	21	22	23	24	25	26
27	28	29	30	31		

August

Mo	Tu	We	Th	Fr	Sa	Su
					1	2
3	4	5	6	7	8	9
10	11	12	13	14	15	16
17	18	19	20	21	22	23
24	25	26	27	28	29	30
31						

September

Mo	Tu	We	Th	Fr	Sa	Su
	1	2	3	4	5	6
7	8	9	10	11	12	13
14	15	16	17	18	19	20
21	22	23	24	25	26	27
28	29	30				

October

Mo	Tu	We	Th	Fr	Sa	Su
			1	2	3	4
5	6	7	8	9	10	11
12	13	14	15	16	17	18
19	20	21	22	23	24	25
26	27	28	29	30	31	

November

Mo	Tu	We	Th	Fr	Sa	Su
						1
2	3	4	5	6	7	8
9	10	11	12	13	14	15
16	17	18	19	20	21	22
23	24	25	26	27	28	29
30						

December

Mo	Tu	We	Th	Fr	Sa	Su
	1	2	3	4	5	6
7	8	9	10	11	12	13
14	15	16	17	18	19	20
21	22	23	24	25	26	27
28	29	30	31			

*Contact us directly to get some cute **free stickers** for your new planner (UK only)!*

Thanks for being an awesome customer!
May your day be filled with sunshine, rainbows and unicorns!

Mirela A S Tipping

Email: Milexis.Kreative.Studio@gmail.com

Instagram: Milexis_Kreative_Studio

Ingram Content Group UK Ltd.
Milton Keynes UK
UKHW020949100723
424832UK00011B/78